RED TAIL

A TUSKEGEE AIRMAN'S RENDEZVOUS WITH DESTINY

CAPT. ROBERT L. MARTIN
WITH KAREN PATTERSON

RED TAIL
A Tuskegee Airman's Rendezvous with Destiny

iUniverse books may be ordered through booksellers or by contacting:

iUniverse
1663 Liberty Drive
Bloomington, IN 47403
www.iuniverse.com
844-349-9409

ISBN: 978-1-6632-5701-7 (sc)
ISBN: 978-1-6632-5700-0 (e)

Library of Congress Control Number: 2023920051

Print information available on the last page.

iUniverse rev. date: 02/26/2024

To all the brave men and women who fought tyranny worldwide
while being denied the rights of full citizenship here at home

CONTENTS

Preface..ix

Acknowledgments xi

Night and Day.. xiii

Introduction xv

Chapter 1   Failure is Not an Option 1

Chapter 2   I Was Going to Be a Pilot.. 19

Chapter 3   I Wanted a Fighter... 35

Chapter 4   Combat Training 57

Chapter 5   Trip to War 70

Chapter 6   I Am in the War! 88

Chapter 7   Mission to Memmingen... 107

Chapter 8   Shot Down over Yugoslavia.. 120

Chapter 9   Tito's Partisans 127

Chapter 10 Back to Ramitelli 138

Epilogue 153

Afterword 165

To One Who Went That Way 169

Bibliography 171

Glossary 173

PREFACE

I first met Robert Martin in February 2012 when he came to St. Andrew for Black History Month. He had just turned ninety-three. He didn't give a speech; that was delivered by Ken Rapier, president of the Chicago "DODO" Chapter of Tuskegee Airmen Inc. But when Captain Martin stood to be introduced, he received a standing ovation. We all recognized the remarkable achievement of this unpretentious man, yet we couldn't know about everything he had encountered and overcome during his lifetime.

Bob Martin and his beautiful wife, Odette, came to our church at the invitation of our dear friends Vern and Jean Duncan. Vern had flown planes off an aircraft carrier in the Pacific Ocean during World War II. As my husband was flying his own Cessna 172, Jean and Vern thought we would be especially interested to meet Bob Martin on a more personal level. Of course, they were right. They invited us to dinner with him partly so the three pilots could swap stories, but mostly we wanted to hear more about Mr. Martin's remarkable life.

When we continued our visit after dinner, I asked whether Mr. Martin had thought about putting his experiences into writing. It turned out that he had already written several short stories about various aspects of his experience. He also had notes from speeches he had given, whether because of an honor bestowed on him or because he had addressed the local chapter of Tuskegee Airmen Inc. or told the story of the Tuskegee Airmen to local schoolchildren. Now, however, he thought it was too late to get his story out to the world in book form.

"Maybe not," I said. I had studied English at a graduate level and had published a short story or two. I volunteered to see whether we could pull Mr. Martin's work together and publish it even though I had no experience in writing books. Over the next six years, it was my great honor to meet regularly with him to discuss his varied life experiences. I was so in awe of him that I couldn't call him "Bob," as he requested ("Robert" was his son), but our formal relationship grew into one of trust and deep affection on both sides, I think, as he revealed more about his life. I lost a very special friend when he passed away at the age of ninety-nine.

Finishing Robert Martin's book has been a priority of mine for many years. Because I could not do this project halfway, it took much longer than originally anticipated. Finally, though, at long last, it is here. I have organized and polished Mr. Martin's entertaining stories and speeches and the many hours of interviews we had. I have also filled in a few gaps from other sources.

Please forgive any lapses in memory or understanding, as most of these events happened a long time ago. I believe the strength of Captain Robert L. Martin's character is evident in these pages and that he would be proud of the finished work. I hope you enjoy it.

Karen Patterson
Homewood, Illinois, 2023

ACKNOWLEDGMENTS

I am profoundly grateful to all those who helped make this project a reality: to Mark Wurl for early story edits, organization, and enthusiasm; to Anne Brady and Tom Dascenzo, who offered a couple more set of eyes; to Kimberly Edwards for interview transcriptions; to my daughter, Audrey, for her advice; to Vinita Hampton Wright for her editing expertise; to the Martin family for their kind invitations to related events and for their invaluable assistance with material, photos, and fact-checking; and to my husband, Noel, for his endless patience, wisdom, and encouragement. Others have also assisted with this project in various ways through the years and in the final publication. I thank you all. This project would not have been what it is today without your assistance.

Karen Patterson
Homewood, Illinois, 2023

NIGHT AND DAY

(Abbreviated)

Night and day, day and night.
Is one of them wrong, and the other one right?
Day is most powerful, causing live things to grow,
But night works its magic; it can hide things, you know.

Fantastic this difference, its effect on us all;
The entire world turns from daybreak to nightfall.
"Dawn comes up like thunder," makes a soldier recall;
Night quietly steals away, can bring peace to us all.

But there lies a great problem
That makes us uptight.
At night it's quite difficult
To tell red from white.

Day and night, it is hard to make choices
When out of the void come so many voices
To say they alone know the very best way
For life to be great, loving both night and day!

—Robert L. Martin, June 2012

INTRODUCTION

In the fall of 1925, the US Army War College sent to the chief of staff a memo that suggested a plan for the use of Black recruits in "the next war." The supporting study drew heavily on prevailing biases. It claimed, among other things, that a Black man was "of inferior mentality ... weak in character ..." and that he had "not the initiative and resourcefulness of the white man."[1] No matter that these assumptions had long been proven false. The self-sacrificing courage during the Civil War of the all-Black Fifty-fourth Massachusetts Infantry Regiment, so vividly on display in the 1989 movie *Glory*, should have laid these claims to rest once and for all. Instead, Black soldiers found that they had to prove themselves all over again during each new conflict, their previous valor and resourcefulness conveniently forgotten. Predictably, the new plan, based on old stereotypes, became US War Department policy during World War II.

The mobilization plan in the war college memo suggested a quota system allowing for approximately 170,000 Black recruits. Roughly 140,000 of them would be assigned to noncombatant duty, which would leave only about 30,000 for the "experiment" of combat duty.[2] And for those not recruited at all, the memo noted that "the majority of negroes left at home will be in the southern states, where they will be needed for

---

[1] "Notes on Proposed Plan for Use of Negro Manpower," point 2, *Memorandum for the Chief of Staff*, November 10, 1925, https://www.fdrlibrary.org/documents/356632/390886/tusk_doc_a.pdf/4693156a-8844-4361-ae17-03407e7a3dee; "Memorandum for the Chief of Staff," Section III, point 1, October 30, 1925, https://www.fdrlibrary.org/documents/356632/390886/tusk_doc_a.pdf/4693156a-8844-4361-ae17-03407e7a3dee, 4.

[2] "Notes on Proposed Plan for Use of Negro Manpower," point 7, *Memorandum for the Chief of Staff*, November 10, 1925, https://www.fdrlibrary.org/documents/356632/390886/tusk_doc_a.pdf/4693156a-8844-4361-ae17-03407e7a3dee.

labor and where they can best be handled by competent whites."[3] This, sixty years after the end of the Civil War! The persistent attitude of white superiority also fostered a pattern of intimidation. This included low-key strategies such as antiloitering laws aimed at recovering a Black labor force through "community service." The ultimate form of intimidation, lynching, continued as well.

The war college could have been called willfully ignorant about the combat abilities of Black soldiers. Leaders tended to focus more on their mistakes in World War I than on their successes, but some of the subpar performance was real—and the army failed to explore the real reasons for it. These troops lacked adequate equipment, training, and support, but it was easy in 1925 to blame any failures on genetics.

Military leaders in 1940 intended to follow the flawed assessment of the war college and limit Black contributions once again. They had no intention of allowing Black recruits into the fledgling air corps. Benjamin O. Davis Jr., having endured four years of silencing at West Point, became its first Black graduate since 1889 when he received his commission and degree in 1936. In spite of his physical fitness and his brilliant academic performance, he was denied admittance into the US Army Air Corps in 1935. Leadership certainly did not intend to allow a Black officer to command white troops, and the air corps did not plan to include any Black units.[4]

Black leaders had other plans. In the twenty years since the end of World War I, prominent spokespeople had advocated greater inclusion of people of color in the military. Black newspapers, including the *Chicago Defender* and the *Pittsburgh Courier*, promoted stories related to aviation. They made heroes of aviation pioneers within the community and kept up pressure for fair representation in the military.[5] Black publishers and editors, such as Robert Vann of the *Courier*, recognized that Blacks had to be included in the emerging field of aviation or they would be left behind again.[6]

---

[3] "Notes on Proposed Plan for Use of Negro Manpower," point 8, *Memorandum for the Chief of Staff*, November 10, 1925, https://www.fdrlibrary.org/documents/356632/390886/tusk_doc_a.pdf/4693156a-8844-4361-ae17-03407e7a3dee.

[4] Benjamin O. Davis Jr., *American: An Autobiography* (New York: Plume, 1992), 44.

[5] Lawrence P. Scott and William M. Womack Sr., *Double V: the Civil Rights Struggle of the Tuskegee Airmen* (East Lansing: Michigan State University Press, 1998), 64–65.

[6] Scott and Womack, *Double V*, 72, 83.

Cornelius Coffey and John Robinson were two aviation pioneers who had found ways around the prevailing bigotry to learn how to fly.[7] In the mid-1930s, they founded an aeronautical association and an aviation school with the aim of increasing Black interest in, and access to, aviation. Civil rights activists such as Walter White, A. Philip Randolph, and Judge William H. Hastie also applied social and political pressure for the inclusion of Blacks in aviation.

All these factions together demanded that the War Department test its assumptions and, with an election approaching and the Black vote at stake, the pressure for equality in the armed forces finally worked. By October 1940, President Roosevelt had issued an announcement that the new air corps was committed to admitting and training Black pilots.[8] In 1941, Captain Davis was released from his other military duties so he could receive pilot training. Once that was completed, he would become the commander of this new unit, which would become known as the 99th Pursuit Squadron.

For this "experiment," a new training base was constructed in cooperation with historically Black Tuskegee University. The program used university facilities while remaining separate from the civilian student body. It included its own Black instructors, technicians, and support personnel. Only the advanced instruction officers on the new army base were white, per war college specifications. This all-Black training base in the Deep South, surrounded by a deeply prejudiced culture, was essentially cut off from the rest of the world. The War Department furnished it with used equipment, and it strictly limited the number of recruits admitted there. Failure of this experiment, it seemed, was predetermined.

Davis completed his pilot training and graduated at Tuskegee along with four other men in March 1942, with other classes following after. These first graduates of the flight program at Tuskegee remained stateside far longer than their white counterparts. When the 99th Pursuit Squadron was finally deployed overseas, its members were, at first, denied the opportunity to prove themselves in combat. Then they were rated poorly for not having proven themselves. Eventually, however, the 99th had their chance to see combat at Pantelleria, Italy. Their subsequent performance at

---

[7]   Scott and Womack, *Double V*, 44.

[8]   Scott and Womack, *Double V*, 137.

Anzio put to rest all doubts as to their ability, and the fabled 99th Pursuit Squadron secured its place in history.[9]

The 99th and the other fighter squadrons of the 332nd Fighter Group that followed—the 100th, the 301st, and the 302nd—were eventually given a job that others were not handling well. Other fighter pilots had been easily lured away from the bombers they were assigned to protect in search of the "kills" that would glorify them as aces. Then other German fighter planes would move in and shoot down their prey. Finally, when bomber losses had risen to unacceptable levels and the morale of bomber crews had plummeted, the 332nd—the Tuskegee Airmen—were given the job. Their orders were simply to stay with the bombers and keep them from being shot down. They did that. With longer tours of duty and fewer replacement pilots than other units had, they turned in a record of bomber protection better than that of their white counterparts. They did their job and thus forever changed the way the US War Department could view Black servicemen.

The legend of the "Red Tails," as they became known because of the distinctive way they marked their planes, was that they never lost a single bomber to enemy aircraft. That is not quite true. The 332nd Fighter Group lost twenty-seven bombers to enemy fighters, by best counts. That's *total*, in the Tuskegee Airmen's entire World War II experience, compared to average losses of forty-six bombers by other fighter groups flying cover for the Fifteenth Air Force. Fifteen of those twenty-seven Red Tail losses happened on a single mission on July 18, 1944, when they encountered an estimated three hundred German fighters. On that day they also lost three pilots, but they shot down eleven enemy aircraft, a Red Tails single-day record.[10]

---

9   Robert A. Rose, *Lonely Eagles: The Story of America's Black Air Force in World War II* (Los Angeles: Tuskegee Airmen Inc., 1996), 60–65.

10   Altogether it is estimated that the Red Tails shot down 119 enemy fighters. They also destroyed radar installations, barges, trains, planes on the ground, and even a destroyer, flying at altitudes too low and too dangerous for bombers. Of the 992 pilots graduated at Tuskegee, an estimated 355 were deployed overseas, 66 were killed in action, and 32 became prisoners of war. They earned, among them, an estimated 744 Air Medal and Clusters awards, 14 Bronze Stars, 150 Distinguished Flying Crosses, and 8 Purple Hearts (Rose, *Lonely Eagles*, 156).

Regarding their achievement, Captain Martin said, "The overall record of the Red Tails was not the work of a single hotshot pilot; it was accomplished by teamwork. The combined operation of sixty-four to seventy-two disciplined Tuskegee Airmen fighter pilots doing their job protected a bomber group of 124 to 163 planes. The 332nd Fighter Group flew a total of 311 missions, 179 of them as cover for the Fifteenth Air Force. We encountered enemy aircraft on thirty-five of those missions, meaning that thirty-five times we *actually* protected 124 to 163 bombers from being shot down. This amounted to a total of about five thousand bombers saved.

"Each of those bombers, which cost about $250,000 at the time, carried ten men: two pilots trained at a cost of $150,000 each, navigation and bombardier officers trained at $100,000 each, and six enlisted crew members trained at a cost of $25,000 each. The total cost in dollars for a lost bomber was, therefore, around $900,000. Contrast that with the cost of a single $45,000 fighter plane and a pilot whose training cost $75,000. War is never economical, but it has economics. The real savings, however, was in the lives of those ten American airmen. That bomber and crew could fly another day. Those ten men, saved, could return home and have children, who could then help repay the war debt. The conscientious support of the Tuskegee Airmen saved about fifty thousand lives. The morale of bomber crews went way up as losses subsided. The Red Tails' reputation grew. Some bomber groups began to ask for us specifically."

Were the Red Tails really that good? In 1948, President Truman ordered the integration of the armed services, and this began with the newly formed US Air Force. Before desegregation was actually achieved, however, the air force held its first ever aerial gunnery competition in the spring of 1949. A team from the 332nd attended with their World War II-era planes and won top honors. Thus, Tuskegee Airmen were actually the first "Top Guns."[11]

---

[11] The US Air Force became a separate branch of the military in 1947. On July 26, 1948, President Truman issued an executive order to desegregate the armed services as quickly as was practical. The first air force gunnery competition was held in Las Vegas on May 2–12, 1949, before desegregation had been completed. A team from the 332nd consisting of Captain Alva Temple, Lieutenant James Harvey, Lieutenant Harry Stewart, and team alternate Lieutenant Halbert Alexander won top team honors. Charles E. Francis, *Tuskegee Airmen: The Men Who Changed a Nation* (Boston: Brandon Books, 2008), 229. These men were the first Top Gun winners,

First Place 1949 Commemoration Plaque.
Presented January 11, 2022.

"Charles Lindbergh once stated," Martin continued, "that he believed aviation was solely the province of the white man. Lindbergh was wrong. The Army War College memo of 1925 was also wrong—on all counts. The Tuskegee Airmen blazed the proof of that across the heavens like a meteor."

But even before World War II, anyone who wanted to know the truth could have. Consider the stories of Eugene Bullard, a Black fighter pilot who served in France during World War I because he was not allowed to fly for the United States; Bessie Coleman, a young Black woman who had to go to Europe to earn her pilot's license in 1921; Walter Madison, a Black citizen of Ames, Iowa, who, in 1912, was granted patent #1,047,098 for a

---

yet no one applauded their victory at the time. Their trophy disappeared for fifty-five years, and winners of that initial competition were listed as "unknown." In the 1990s, records of the meet were found and the true winners officially acknowledged. The trophy was finally discovered in a storage area in 2004 [reportedly in a box marked "Do Not Open"]. Stephen Losey, "Meet the First 'Top Guns,'" *Military Officers Association of America*, May 23, 2022, https://www.moaa.org/content/publications-and-media/news-articles/2022-news-articles/meet-the-first-top-guns/.

flying machine. Black people had already proven that aviation was as much their field as anyone else's.

But there is more. "When the story of the Tuskegee Airmen is told," Martin resumed, "I want people to know about our success as military men as well as pilots. A squadron is supposed to be led by a colonel, or at least a 'light' [lieutenant] colonel, and he didn't get there yesterday. He worked his way up through the ranks of lieutenant, then captain, then major, before he became a colonel. We did not have anyone groomed to step in as squadron leaders. Our squadron leaders were first or second lieutenants chosen out of the pilots' ranks. These men had demonstrated superior ability as leaders and were then appointed to lead by Colonel Davis, who commanded the entire fighter group.

"These men took up the reins and performed. Within a year's time after getting their commissions, they were in command positions. They were leading groups on missions. The bomber outfits had a navigator in every ship, and they had a lead navigator. We had a first lieutenant leading a sixty-four- or seventy-two-plane group to meet our bombers at a calculated rendezvous point someplace high over the German-held territories of central Europe. Here were men with the rank of platoon leaders leading squadrons. The ability was there, and they performed. They performed very well.

"You might ask why Black people would want to fight for a country that treated us as second-class citizens, that hadn't given us opportunities for leadership. We had to fight for our civil rights at home at the same time we were fighting the enemy abroad. But what might Hitler have done to us? Better to fight him over there than here. Besides, what other country were we going to fight for? Black people have developed this country just as much as anyone else who came here. Our blood went into the soil where we worked crops. Our minds went into all the fields of engineering and government needed by this country."

Look at mathematician and astronomer Benjamin Banneker. Look at Booker T. Washington, author, educator, and advisor to US presidents, who was born into slavery and went on to found Tuskegee Institute. Look at Dr. George Washington Carver, the scientist and inventor dubbed by *Time* magazine in 1941 a "Black Leonardo."

"Yes," Martin concluded, "our country has treated us like second-class citizens, but this is still our country; here we have made our mark. We don't owe our allegiance to any African nation. German Americans, Irish Americans—even in their second generation in this country, some of them carry allegiance to a place they might never have visited. I pledge allegiance to this nation because it's the one I know."

What follows is Captain Martin's story as he told it to me.

Karen Patterson
Homewood, Illinois, 2023

CHAPTER 1

FAILURE IS NOT AN OPTION

My father's father was born into slavery. Ambrose Martin came of age in rural Louisiana sometime after the emancipation of 1863. He made his living transporting goods and passengers with a team of horses and a wagon. Ambrose was known as a good horseman, but around 1886 he decided to take a job as a mail carrier—even though he had never been taught to read. How was he to make sense of the names and addresses on the mail he was supposed to deliver? Like the survivor he was, he found a way.

Ambrose Martin.

My father, Henry Martin, found a way to support his family when factory jobs in Dubuque were closed to people of color. Most Black people in town were forced to live in horribly substandard segregated housing, but my father made sure we had a decent roof over our heads.

Like my father and grandfather before me, I knew education was the key to a better life. My grandfather did not know how to read, but his twelve-year-old son did. They split the postal route. Henry read his father's share to him, and father and son delivered the mail to their respective territories on horseback in rural Louisiana. When Henry, my father, needed a better income to support his own growing family, he knew he had to go back to school. And as my mother lay dying of peritonitis from a burst appendix when I was just six months old, my father promised that all her children would be well educated. This was something that no one would ever be able to take away from us.

My father was true to his word. Altogether, he raised nine children, and each of us earned at least a bachelor's degree. Six of the nine earned advanced degrees too.

I was my parents' sixth child, born on February 9, 1919. My mother, Mattie Ducano (pronounced DOO-kan-oh), had grown up on her family's farm in Belcher, Louisiana. Belcher is a village ninety-four miles northwest of Natchitoches, where a similar name, Ducaurnau, is still known.

The story told is that a man by the name of Ducaurnau emigrated from Pau, France, in 1806, not long after the French had sold the Louisiana Territory to the United States. Mr. Ducaurnau had a business and held slaves. One of his slaves, Ellen Larkin, bore him a son who went by the name of Charlie Ducano.

It is said that Mr. Ducaurnau arranged freedom for all his slaves upon his death. In addition, he granted one hundred acres of farmland to each of the women who had borne him children. Charlie, who thus became a landed free man when he grew up, eventually took over management of his family's farm. In due time, he married Mary Jane Marks, a free woman. I am not certain of the generation, but my mother, Mattie Ducano, was a descendant of Charlie and Mary Jane. She was born in 1887, the eldest of her siblings. In 1919, after my mother died, my father buried her in the family cemetery on the farm on which she had grown up.

My father's father, Ambrose Martin, met and married a woman by the name of Hettie Porter. Together they started a family in Many, Louisiana, a tiny town just thirty miles from Natchitoches. My father was born in 1874. He also had two sisters: Lelia, who was the oldest, and Rosetta. It was probably here that my father and his own father partnered to deliver mail.

My father, standing in center, with sisters Lelia (left) and Rosetta (right). Seated in front are their father, Ambrose Martin (left) and their mother, Hetti Porter Martin (right), with Lelia's daughter Claudia standing between them.

My grandfather eventually moved his family to Natchitoches, a cotton-shipping town and home to the school founded there in 1884 that would become Northwestern State University of Louisiana. In Natchitoches, my grandfather settled his family into a small shotgun-style house with a wooden picket fence, a shaded front porch, and a barn with pastureland out back.

Mattie was an elementary schoolteacher when my father met her, presumably in Natchitoches.

My mother, Mattie Ducano Martin.

They married and began their family with my brother Henry, who was born in 1908. Henry was soon followed by Clarence, Lillian, and Vivian. Then my father was injured on the job.

Around the turn of the twentieth century, rivers were a common way to travel and carry trade goods. The Red River, which runs past Natchitoches, was important for trade. Unfortunately, heavy rains often caused erosion of the riverbanks, allowing trees to fall into the water and create logjams. Even if the channel looked clear, a snag, a dead tree hidden in the water, could catch on a boat, rip a hole in its hull, and sink it, spelling disaster for both passengers and owners. The solution was to have so-called snag boats travel the river just to get the trees out of the water and clear the waterways.

Henry, my father, worked on the Red River and other rivers in the South. He and his crew even followed the Mississippi River as far north as Dubuque. At Dubuque, probably around 1914, a barrel or drum of some sort got out of control on the dock. It fell against my father when he could not get out of the way in time, and the impact of it tore the skin off his shins. He was taken to the hospital, but doctors there were unable to help him much. The skin never grew back properly. My father would spend the rest of his life dressing and redressing his skinned shins. If these wounds continued to cause him pain, he never admitted it, but the injury did mean he could no longer work on the snag boats.

Dubuque had plenty of industry. Having started out as a lead mining town, it was home to a company during the Civil War that made lead shot by dropping molten lead from a tower through a screen so it could fall to the ground as tiny pellets. By the twentieth century, however, Dubuque was known primarily as a lumber town. It had the largest sash and door manufacturing companies in the world, and the Brunswick factory in Dubuque built elaborate bars that were in demand in taverns around the world. Dubuque Star Brewery had also set up operations there. In addition, Dubuque's location on the Mississippi River made it a premier shipping hub, and the Dubuque Boat and Boiler Works built tugboats and other boats for use on the river.

There were certainly plenty of jobs to fill. Even so, none of Dubuque's industries had made room for Black workers. There was no need for them even to apply. The only work my father could find in Dubuque after his injury was that of a porter in a barbershop. He swept floors, among other things, and may have done a few other odd jobs to bring in money, but this was hardly enough for a family of six.

It was at this juncture that my father met Dr. Henry Rose. Dr. Rose was a chiropodist, a foot doctor, and he encouraged Dad to study chiropody. At that time, feet were considered dirty, which meant there were few white people willing to care for them. People in Dubuque, white by an overwhelming majority, went to Black chiropodists to get their corns, calluses, and toenails cut, and to have their warts treated and their orthotics fitted. Chiropodists could do anything needed for the relief of aching feet except operate under the skin, and they were in demand. A person could make a good living doing what others would not.

Inspired by Dr. Rose, my father traveled to Chicago to enter Moeller Chiropody College while his family remained in the South. Henry and Clarence, then ages eight and six, were helping my mother's father on the farm in Belcher. Lillian and Vivian lived with our Aunt Rosetta in Natchitoches.

My father passed all of his exams and graduated from chiropody college around 1916. Then he returned to Dubuque to open an office. Later, in 1917, he and Mattie were blessed with Hettie's birth. I arrived eighteen months later, but when my mother died, my father was forced to adjust his long-term plans. He was eventually able to purchase a family home close to his downtown office, but conditions for bringing the family together in Dubuque proved unfavorable for a few more years.

Frank and Rosetta Brown at home in Natchitoches with
my sisters Vivian (left) and Lillian (right), 1921.

My mother's mother came to take care of Hettie and me for a year or two.
Then Mrs. Lelia McClelland, my father's older sister, came. I knew her as
my beloved Aunt Missie. I never felt deprived of a mother's love.

When I was six, Aunt Missie and I took the train south to Natchitoches
for my Grandpa Ambrose's funeral. I was small for my age, so I had been
told to tell anybody who asked that I was five so I could ride for free. I was
a rather bright child, however, and I could do things I should not have been
able to do. This caused the conductor to ask my age several times, but I
never forgot the age I was supposed to be throughout that long trip. And
the trip was long. There was a rumor that the crew kept stopping the train
so they could pick wild strawberries and other fruit on that slow journey
through Arkansas, and I couldn't have proven otherwise!

Natchitoches was warm and flowery, very different from Dubuque.
I did not venture off to explore it, though. The cemetery was old and
creepy, the tombstones engraved with French names I couldn't pronounce.
The house next door to Grandpa's had a big lot surrounded by a white
picket fence, which was covered with climbing rosebushes in flower. I don't
remember whether the owner was white or colored, but I do remember
the stern instruction not to pick any of those beautiful flowers. Similarly, I
don't remember whether Aunt Missie and I caught anything when we went
fishing—an outing I can dimly recollect. But what did make an impression
was the need to watch for snakes in the pond and around the berry bushes.

I'm seated in the car. Outside the car are my aunts Lelia (left) and Rosetta (center), and Grandmother Martin (right). 1925.

Lelia's daughter Claudia, Aunt Rosetta, and me in front of my grandfather's house. 1925.

Aunt Missie and I returned to Dubuque soon enough. We had already made that trip the other way around; nothing about our return sticks in my memory.

Sometime around Christmas that year, Lillian and Vivian, now ages thirteen and eleven, arrived from Natchitoches. They began almost immediately to help my father around the house and in his chiropody office. Vivian took me to school on the first day of the spring semester after they arrived. After that, since Vivian and Lillian attended junior high and high school, Hettie took me to school. I was eager to go.

I'm not sure where Clarence lived when my brothers first arrived home from the South, but it was decided that Henry would bunk with me. This was sometime during the great bedbug invasion, when you went to bed knowing you *would* wake up covered with bites. We had no box springs, just springs. Bedbugs would get into the coils along with dust and lint, so the first order of business when Henry arrived was to take a gasoline blowtorch to the springs. Then we fumigated anything else that could be a nesting place for bedbugs. After that, Henry got four-by-fours and angle irons and built bunk beds for the iron springs and two mattresses. This was the only way he and I could share my small bedroom. And I got to sleep on the top bunk!

My dad's mother came to Dubuque shortly after my grandfather's funeral. She and Aunt Missie moved into a house at the top of the hill. They were joined by Missie's daughter, Claudia, who was quite ill and confined to bed. Whatever sickness she had wasn't told to children, but it was not too long before she died. Then Claudia's son, Alonzo, came to live with his grandmother. He was of high school age, the same age as Vivian. I think Clarence may have lived in that household.

Around the same time, in 1925, my father took our family to a huge Ku Klux Klan gathering west of Dubuque. We sat in the car and watched as KKK members burned two or three crosses at the top of a hill. At least some of the white-hooded individuals were likely neighbors, fellow professionals, or patients of my father. He went to show that he was not afraid of them. Soon afterward, I understand, KKK influence began to weaken for a time because of power struggles on the national level, but I like to think that my father may have shamed the local organization just a little too. The KKK was not a major force in my life, but my father's refusal to be intimidated provided an important example for all of us.

There were not enough Black people in Dubuque for us to be totally segregated. Out of a population of about forty thousand at the time, only eighty-eight were listed in the 1920 census as "Negroes." Because there were so few of us, the school system, parks, and playgrounds were not segregated, but businesses and housing were. I was not allowed to eat in certain restaurants in Dubuque. Black travelers were refused hotel accommodations and were forced to seek rooms in the homes of Black families, mine included. I could not patronize a barbershop although I could work in one. In fact, being a barbershop porter seemed to be the only job available to me as a teenager if I didn't choose to work in my father's office.

As a child, I never thought about the restrictions in our lives. Aunt Missie would take me along when she went to buy her clothing, and I remember the satisfaction of having store clerks give me pennies for singing. I loved to sing. In Dubuque, unlike in the South, Aunt Missie could even try on clothes in the store whether she ended up buying them or not.

Dubuque's segregated housing meant that there was only one small area in which most of the Black population could live, and most of that housing was substandard. The exceptions I recall were that John Wells owned a very nice house, my father owned a house that was not in a segregated area of the city, and Mrs. Henrietta Pelkey owned a decent apartment house. Other rentals were of low caliber. One area, in particular, was just plain awful.

Dorothy Pelkey, possibly a niece of Mrs. Henrietta Pelkey, was my first stepmother. A few years before, she and her sister, Elizabeth, both light-skinned women with long hair, had worked at one of the large department stores in downtown Chicago. They had worked as attendants in the ladies' apparel department, helping women into and out of various articles of clothing.

When Elizabeth came to visit Dorothy in Dubuque, I heard them as they came home from the store one day talking about their experience in Chicago and the discrimination they had seen there. At that time, the prices of merchandise were noted in an alphabetic code, which made it easy for the clerks to change the prices of items on certain customers and pocket the difference. Dorothy and Elizabeth knew the code, so they knew that Black customers were being overcharged. This went on for years, by the way, until J. C. Penney came along and hung the prices right on the merchandise. Suddenly it didn't matter who came to look at an item; the price was clear and did not change.

My father married Dorothy in 1927. Their first son, Thornton, was born around Christmas 1928. The girls' room, the biggest bedroom, became Dad's, stepmother Dorothy's, and baby Thornton's room. The three girls were relocated to a new bedroom that had been added across the back side of the house, built over a new attached garage. It was a large, square bedroom with about a dozen windows. The biggest problem was that there was no heat in this room, and of course the garage below was also unheated. A *major* number of quilts and blankets were required in the winter! Sometimes my sisters used an electric heater; a kerosene heater was out of the question because the house was too vulnerable to fire. A minor problem was passing through Dad's bedroom to the centrally located bathroom, but we lived with very little friction due to a strong dictator: Dad.

Nothing is ever perfectly square, especially in Dubuque. Our house on Hill Street was a mess of angles. It seemed there were no perfect right angles. Hill Street was a diagonal road up the bluff from the river valley. The front of the house faced Hill Street but was not perfectly square to it. The south side ran at an angle to the south lot line. The west and south sides of the house came together at a very sharp angle. The house next door was on a level ten feet above ours. A wall of large stones rose gradually from three feet to about ten feet, thereby creating a narrowing passageway to the backyard. We could pass through easily, however—until one day the wall burst outward, pushing the large stones into the wall of our dining room.

My boyhood home.

On the north side of the house was a steep driveway. We got a Model T Ford and parked it in the backyard until the new garage was built. The gas tank was located under the dashboard, and there was no pump, so when the car was low on gas, we had to drive it backward up the hill to park it.

Near the front of the house was a basement window through which fuel was delivered for the furnace. We used coke, a superior fuel derived from coal. Delivery men carried it, sack by sack, and fed it through the basement window into the coal bin. An unfortunate hedge stood in the way of their progress; it was always trampled as the men walked back and forth.

The man across the street from us owned a floral nursery, and on Mother's Day, my father bought each of us a white carnation. He bought a red one for the current wife if she had any children. Besides his own house, the man with the nursery had built three houses on our block for his children, each one higher than the next. Our dentist, Dr. Leach, lived on the same block. A little farther back was where Bobby, my autistic (in today's terminology, probably schizophrenic) playmate lived. These families were all white. Yet we obviously lived there too. The segregation evident in other parts of Dubuque did not seem to apply in our neighborhood.

Our family members continued to arrive from the South. My Aunt Rosetta Brown, my father's younger sister, came when I was about eleven years old. She moved into a house about halfway up the hill. When she wanted to make ice cream, I had to get into my wagon and ride it to the bottom of the hill, buy a twenty-five-pound chunk of ice, and haul it up the hill. Then I had to chop it up and turn the handle, which was not an easy chore. Then, after all that work, I did not even get to lick the dasher! To this day, I do not like homemade ice cream.

Dorothy had two more children, Delores and Joe, before she died in 1932. After she passed away, my father married three or four more times. He married Lulu Adkins from Chicago in 1933. He married Mabel Rose from Grand Rapids, Michigan, around 1939. That marriage did not work out; my father took Mabel back to Michigan in 1940. I was in college at the time. Then, late in 1944, when I was in Italy, one of the members of the squadron came up to me and said, "Your father just got married!" It turned out that, at the age of seventy, he had married a relative of this guy, a woman by the name of Susie Hart. My father had not even told us.

Henry A. Martin's chiropody office was in the Security Building, in the heart of Dubuque at Eighth and Main, where he had an all-white practice. It was perfectly situated between the German community on the north side of town and the Irish community on the south side. Our neighbor, Dr. Leach, had his dental practice on the same floor as my father's office. Now I wonder how my father managed to get an office right in the middle of downtown. What did he have to do to get such a prime location? I never worried about those things when I was growing up. Dad was very well respected in the community and was a Master Mason, so he obviously had his connections.

My father held office hours six and a half days a week, but sometimes on Sunday afternoons we would drive out to the countryside so he could buy gas. He also used this time to drum up business and get his name out. He would pass out his business cards and buy ice-cream cones for the kids who came along. I think I was usually the one who went with him.

Afterward, people could say, "The doctor came out and bought some gas, said hello, and told us what he might be able to do for us."

In addition, we would find telephone poles at a few road intersections, tack up about fifty flyers with a nail, and go on our way. I have no idea how much business this effort earned my father, but surely some farmers with foot problems came to see him. At any rate, I enjoyed those two- or three-hour outings with my father.

Dad was flexible enough to accept barter for his services when needed. A farmer might travel into town during the week and come up to see him and say, "Look, Doc, my feet are killing me. I haven't got any money, but I've got a couple dozen eggs out in my car." Or maybe he had a chicken or two, or a side of bacon, and he'd say, "Well, Doc, can you take a look and see what's wrong?"

My father would say, "Sure!" Barter could help feed a family for a week or more. He was charging two dollars for a foot treatment, but he was amicable. If you can get people to talk to you, it's amazing how much you can get done together.

When I was about four years old, sometimes I would leave the house and walk part of the way to my dad's office. Then, usually, I would turn around and walk straight home. But sometimes I sneaked away to the home of my friend, Joe Gibbs, who lived on Rock Street. This would give Aunt

Missie a big scare. Rock Street was not a place where anybody should have wanted to be.

The merchant barons on the north side of Dubuque built large homes on the river bluff that extends northward about five miles. The idea was to build above anybody else so you could see beyond them, and today these mansions are great tourist attractions. The housing on Rock Street was built onto the bluff too, but in no other way was it even remotely similar.

Joe's family was poorer than dirt poor. The units on Rock Street were nothing more than a few bare wooden two- and three-story hovels. This unbelievable place chopped into the bluff and attached to the rocks had no electricity, no running water, no paint, no plaster—nothing. The units, three stories high and stepped back as they rose up the bluff, had "outhouses" built onto the backs of them. Can you imagine a three-story outhouse? It could only work because the higher units overhung the lower ones in back, meaning that the effluent from the upper stories fell behind each lower one.

Many years later, when a Tuskegee Airman friend of mine asked about Rock Street, I wanted to disappear into the cracks. He said, "My father came to Dubuque and met my mother. She lived on Rock Street. My father took her back to Des Moines, where I was born and raised."

I didn't want to take this man to see that place, whatever might be left of it. I knew that my friend's mother might have lived in the part where Joe Gibbs's family lived, before we came along. I believe that more than one hardworking family must have lived in that horrible place. I evaded the question and let it go at that.

The Gibbs family would come to Dubuque in the summertime to find whatever work they could find and make some money while crops were growing on the farm in the south. They would go back to harvest in the fall, spend the winter in the south, and work the farm early in the spring. Then they would return to Dubuque, to bare-bones walls and floors attached to the side of the cliff—stacked migrant worker shacks.

I don't know what Joe and I played when I visited there, but we scrambled around the rocks and must have enjoyed each other's company. That adventure ended in later years when Joe was sent south each summer to find work. But when we did play together on Rock Street, I remember coming home to Aunt Missie's ire. In an effort to cure me of running away, she tied me to the big tree in my front yard with a rope about an inch in diameter so passersby could see and shame me.

A terror of my young life around 1924 was the garbage man, a rough-looking white character who, every time he saw me, threatened to feed me to his bulldogs. Whenever I caught sight of this man, I would run home and into the house screaming. Aunt Missie finally told him to stop threatening me, and she told me that she was going to poison the dogs. One day she announced that she had poisoned the dogs, and I lived in fear no more.

I used to play in the small park diagonally across the street with Bobby, the autistic (or schizophrenic) white boy, under the watchful eye of his mother. She allowed us to play together only when Bobby was in his best mood. I was told that when he became upset, he had the strength of a thirteen-year-old and would hurt me terribly, on purpose, if he could get his hands on me. When Bobby got upset, I had to go home.

There were only four other Black boys in the city who were about my age. We played together sometimes, but not a lot. Those friends had to work when they got a little older. I didn't have to, so I found other friends or played alone.

My street was in a valley between two hills, so of course it was named Hill Street. When it rained hard, the water sometimes spanned the street from curb to curb. When I was older, around ten or eleven years old, I had a great time playing in the stream of rushing water. Luckily, no broken bottles came through to cut my legs. The park across the street was, of course, another great place to play. It had a gently sloping area for playing softball and steeper slopes for riding sleds and skiing in the winter.

As I grew older, I played with children who lived farther down the hill. They were German or Slavic. We played kick the can, red rover, softball, and dodgeball. In the winter, we played hockey on the packed icy surface of the ball field. We found other fun things to do too. There was snow to be shoveled and streets for our sleds to slide down when traffic was light. Several streets in this hilly river town were too steep and dangerous for sledding, but on some occasions, we would walk three or four miles to get a long ride down the slope of Kaufman Avenue, where there were few cars.

Religion was a part of my young life. We Black people had a church, but it was a dilapidated building located in Robinson Alley, a neglected part of town not far from Rock Street. Hettie and I would walk to Sunday school and place our coins in the collection. Nobody seemed to question the safety of this trip, where the down-and-out were sleeping off their Saturday night excesses.

We had a resident minister then. From the time I was very young, there was a great effort to raise money for a new church. Each year for many years the parishioners would cook chicken and barbecue dinners and serve them in the dining room of a large white Methodist church. Henry and Clarence would help roast a steer, working all night before the day of the special dinner. Parishioners would come from thirty-five miles away to help cook and serve. It was a magnificent effort. Finally, we collected enough money to buy another building.

An existing church building with a parish house, owned by whites, became available for sale, and our church made arrangements to buy it. But when the long-anticipated day arrived and it was time to complete the transaction, neither the minister nor his wife were anywhere to be found. We discovered that they had left town during the night with the money. I was seven or eight years old at the time. I never felt the same again about religion, and our church never again had a resident minister.

A traveling minister came up maybe once a month from Clinton, seventy-five miles away, to preach a sermon. After the service, he and his wife would have dinner with us. Nobody else seemed inclined to hospitality, I guess. The meal was cooked by my sister, my aunt, or my stepmother; you can believe we didn't starve, even during the Depression.

I don't recall ever going up to the altar to swear allegiance and join a church. I knew God was still okay, and I said my prayers at night, but after the experience we went through, I wanted nothing to do with the church and organized religion. How could anyone depend on that? In fact, this church did not survive its betrayal. Like me, other people just lost interest and drifted away.

During the war, when I was in Italy, I attended church services on Sunday nights just to see the movie that followed. Even then I was a reluctant attender. By the time I arrived, the only seats remaining were always right up against the screen.

Other memories were happier. One of the things we used to do in the fall was go on a day-long excursion to a farm that had walnut trees. We would take a couple of gunny sacks with us and bring them back full of walnuts. Then we had to knock off all the husks, staining our hands in the process. You can't wash off walnut stain, so we went to school with stained hands for about a week. We had to wait for the walnuts to dry out, but finally, once they had dried, we could crack them for the fruitcake. We used a section of discarded streetcar rail as an anvil. We would place the nuts on it and hit them with a hammer. Walnut meats were delicious in candy as well as fruitcake, so they were well worth the effort.

At Christmastime, I got to beat the eggs to make eggnog. We didn't have an electric beater, just a hand and a spoon. I could also beat many a 1-2-3-4 cake with an ordinary spoon. I was the family beater—its engine, as it were—for this and other things, including ice cream. Maybe that was just because I was available. I didn't mind making anything but the ice cream.

For the eggnog, I would beat the egg yolks, add the sugar, milk, and cream, and then my father would come down to pour just the right amount of alcohol into the eggnog. I was in my teens one Christmas when we'd beaten the eggnog and my father came down to put the whiskey in. He had a bottle of Hennessey, or something like that.

My brother Joe, nine years old at the time, said, "I don't want any of that Hennessey in my eggnog." He wanted some other brand.

My sister had a fit. She said, "What's the matter, you're going to let this nine-year-old boy choose what kind of alcohol he wants to drink?"

My father just laughed it off. Once a year, the kids got a little alcohol.

Of course we had fun during the holidays, but going to school was also a joy for me. I learned everything, although I did not like reading books. Hettie was a smart girl who always got good grades. I tried to get grades as good as hers all the way through school but didn't quite manage it.

Lillian was probably the smartest of all of us. She consistently had a grade point average that landed her on the student honor roll each marking period, but getting into the National Honor Society was a different matter altogether. Lillian would get honors one marking period, and the next time there would be just enough difference to keep her from the grade point average she needed to be accepted into the NHS. This award would have recognized her as the outstanding high school student she was. She often said her grades were being changed, but how could we have proven that she was denied top honors just because she was "colored"?

I had no desire to be a top student. My siblings were the smart ones; I found I couldn't keep up with them. When we brought our report cards home, mine was always lacking, always having a couple of Bs with the As. My siblings didn't seem to have that problem.

Our family had no monetary rewards for grades, but Dad's "That's good; keep it up" was reward enough.

Hettie and I came home for lunch from grammar school every day and scrounged for whatever lunch we could find. We had peanut butter and jelly or canned soup, among other things. A memory I shall never forget is that of having a can of salmon with a finely chopped onion along with crackers and milk. Then back up the hill to Lincoln School we went.

Hettie contracted scurvy, I think, and it affected the calves of her legs. When I was in third grade, her doctors took her to the State University Hospital in Iowa City for special study and treatment during the summer. She came back in fine shape and started school on the first day. I had no medical troubles except the usual—measles, mumps, and chicken pox. I was vaccinated for smallpox.

Hettie moved off to junior high, but some of her intelligence must have rubbed off on me. In fourth grade, I was promoted one half grade, and in sixth grade I was promoted again. In that sixth-grade year, the class laughed when I pronounced "fatigue" as "fat-e-gue." My explanation was that no one in my family was fatigued; they just got tired! The sixth-grade promotion was different from the one in fourth grade in that five other students moved up with me. We formed a clique that lasted through junior high and into senior high.

As I grew still older, I began to play with boys who lived up the hill. "Up the hill" meant everything. These boys had better homes and nicer clothing, and they had a few pennies to spend. We bought kites to fly above the top of the bluff after school. We didn't have to run with the kite; we just tossed it into the air, and up it would go in the afternoon breeze that rose straight up the bluff. We built scooters from old roller skates and two-by-fours; we built coaster cars using old wagon wheels. These cars had steering wheels to turn the front wheels in the right direction. We didn't race them; we just rolled down a hill on a smooth street with very few autos.

We made guns that shot rubber bands made from automobile inner tubes, and we ambushed passing automobiles. After eight or more rubber bands had hit the side of his car, a motorist would stop to determine the trouble. Then we would run, even though we had shot from ambush. Other times, we made small campfires and roasted potatoes—if we could snitch any from home.

While going to junior high, I got a good pair of skates with only two wheels on each skate. In good weather, I skated uphill, downhill, and up another hill to the promenade walk at the front entrance of the school. There I coasted while unstrapping my skates, grabbed them up, and raced to my homeroom—late so many times. Sometimes I had to stay after school as punishment. Later, when I was a cadet in the air corps, I learned to make formations on time so my class would not get bad marks and punishment.

I remember trying to perfect my writing by using the Palmer method of penmanship. It consisted of filling in paper exercise sheets with writing and long columns of numbers such as an accountant might have to prepare, all while trying to be ever so neat. My fun classes were in manual training, bell wiring, and woodworking shop. In wood shop, we learned to sharpen a blade for a woodworking plane without grinding it into a worthless piece of metal. We learned to operate a wood lathe to create pretty spindles to support a banister rail for a staircase, or the handle and head of a gavel for the director of a meeting. My stepmother never had a club to preside over, but she received a gavel, as did everyone else's mother.

I also learned not to wear loose clothing, such as a tie, when operating a lathe. You might ask how I learned this, and the answer is simple. One day my tie got caught in the work and I had to cut it off in a hurry to save myself from harm. Sometimes the most valuable lessons don't come with grades.

Of course, there were lessons in English and civics and table manners. Some kids had to be taught at this late stage in their lives, but I already knew how to act at the table. Then, finally, after vocational training and academic mastery of the Latin rudiments—"amo, amas, amat"—junior high school was over. I got my first pair of long pants for ninth-grade graduation.

CHAPTER 2

I WAS GOING TO BE A PILOT

I wanted to be a Boy Scout, but when I reached the age for scouting, there was no troop I could join. I was told that when a troop was full, it would accept no extras, white or Black—and it seemed every troop in town was full. One group of people tried to form a new troop so I could be included, but they didn't succeed. That particular mix of people just did not gel, so the effort fell apart.

My brother Henry was friendly with German folks on the north end of town. They had a Sea Scout troop, so since there wasn't a Boy Scout troop I could get into, I tried to join the Sea Scouts. That hope was dashed, however, when the mothers of these boys said openly that if I joined, they would disband the troop. I didn't want to create a big fuss, so I dropped the idea of joining a troop. I did not, however, give up on my dream of becoming a Scout.

The Boy Scouts had created a precedent for kids in places such as Haymarket, South Dakota, where there weren't enough Scouts within sixty miles to form a single troop. Those kids could become Lone Scouts. So, in the city of Dubuque in 1932, where there were white troops but no place for me, I became a Lone Scout. I was thirteen years old.

I had a great time at Scout camp for a week that summer. I slept in a tent with a group, ate in the mess hall, took my turn at KP along with other jobs, played in the pool—everything. But I did not advance to first class, because I could not swim. When I got back from camp, I went to the YMCA every weekday for the rest of the summer and took lessons in all the rudiments of swimming: breathing, turning the head from side to side, and kicking. But something was missing. I still could not swim. I just played in the shallow end of the pool, doing belly flops and floating across. Then one day, I raised my head after floating a while and found I was a foot from the far edge. I stroked down with my arm and reached the side of the pool. I tried again and immediately told myself, "I can swim!" And I could.

Dubuque has a city beach on the Mississippi River complete with lifeguards, a diving platform, float platforms, guard ropes—the works. As I got better at swimming, I left the "Y" and tried to join the best group of swimmers, the ones who lived in summer homes a half mile downstream. Whenever a tugboat with barges went by, creating big waves and whirlpools, these guys would swim out to the middle of the river and ride the waves downstream. Then they would make for their homes on shore.

I never trusted those waves; other swimmers could have that thrill. But swimming across the river, which was about a half mile wide at that point? That I determined to do. To train for it, I swam well out from shore into the current. Once I reached the point where I could swim against the current and stay even with a point on shore, I would practice for an hour at a time to build up my endurance. Finally, when I felt I was ready, I asked my friend Bill to accompany me in a rowboat, and I swam all the way across the Mississippi River. Rite of passage accomplished.

Bill lived half a block from me. His grandfather had been a Union soldier in the Civil War, so when he came to town, Bill insisted that I meet him. I've never been so awed as when I met the man, shook his hand, and listened as he told me something about the war. To meet someone who had faced danger for the benefit of others, and to know that I was one of those beneficiaries, was an honor I cannot begin to describe. Small wonder that Bill, his grandson, was the type of kid to whom I felt I could entrust my life when swimming alone across the mighty Mississippi. He was never more than five yards away from me the whole time.

I had to go through the scouting experience largely alone, but there were exceptions. When all the Boy Scouts in the city were recruited to guard the airfield for an air show, this Lone Scout was not excluded. We sat on the edge of the field and kept the crowds from getting in the way of the airplanes. We performed our job well, and we even got to see a pilot set a world record for outside loops. I spent the whole day there.

After the air show was over, airplane rides were offered for two dollars a person. I ran home and somehow persuaded my father to drive me back to the airport with my three sisters and buy us a ride in a real airplane. I was excited. This was going to be something!

Courteous Scout that I was, I let my sisters get on first. I was the last one to board. The plane was a Ford Trimotor, which carried ten passengers. The only seat left by the time I got on was up front in the copilot's seat. What good luck! I got strapped into my seat, as happy as could be.

When the pilot got all three engines going, he reached up and pulled down an electric wire hooked to the ceiling of the plane. *What*, I wondered, *could that be for?*

The pilot touched that live wire to my shoulder, and it shocked the heck out of me. I jerked hard against my safety belt, but the belt held me in place; I wasn't going anywhere. The pilot, not seeming to notice my distress, announced, "You are gonna be a pilot!"

Whether this was supposed to be some sort of initiation or was just what it seemed, a cruel stunt, I do not know. I do know that once we finally took off, I was mesmerized. The ride above the city was fantastic. It was a real thrill to view all of Dubuque laid out at my feet, to see things I hadn't known existed and other things I did know about but now could experience from a whole different perspective. I could see the tiny clock tower and the whole downtown area. I could recognize some streets even though I couldn't find my house. I was not allowed to handle any of the controls, but when we got home, that airplane ride was all I could think or talk about. I was hooked.

The next spring, I attended my brother Henry's graduation from the University of Michigan at Ann Arbor. Henry had earned his degree in chemical engineering and had made friends in many parts of the engineering campus. He got special permission for me to watch a wind tunnel test in which the aeronautical engineering students were experimenting with a new high-speed airfoil. An airfoil looks like a miniature airplane wing. The one I saw was suspended from wires inside the wind tunnel. These wires were connected to scales that could measure various reactions and pressures during the test.

The huge fans were turned on; the wind noise roared louder and louder and then settled into a smooth, loud hum. Onlookers could watch through the small observation window, but all one could see was the airfoil dimly illuminated and suspended there in the three-hundred-mile-per-hour wind that blew through the test chamber.

Today, after my pilot experiences, three hundred miles per hour seems like a foot-dragging walking pace, but in 1933, watching that in a wind tunnel was like seeing Buck Rogers going to Saturn at rocket speed. At the end of the test, the fans were turned off and, after a time, the noise died down. Had the airfoil moved? How far? How much lift was generated? The recorders told it all. This was some fantastic stuff.

Later that day, when I saw my dad, I blurted out, "Dad, I want to be an aeronautical engineer!"

"No, Son," my father said gently. "There are no jobs for a colored aeronautical engineer."

I felt the sting of disappointment as the truth of his words sank in, but I did have a hard-earned promise to fall back onto. "I'm gonna be a pilot, anyway," I said. No one could dash that hope for me. After all, it had been foretold by the pilot with the electric wire.

It should be noted that our trip to Henry's graduation was memorable for another reason. After the ceremony, Henry wanted to drive east from Ann Arbor to see his girlfriend in Detroit, and once there, we realized we were hungry.

Sometimes the security of the known can provide false assurance in the unknown. Sometimes when you are vulnerable, the world reaches out and slaps you in the face. We stopped at a White Castle to get something to eat and waited our turn along with other customers who clearly could get anything on the menu they were willing to pay for. I knew exactly what I wanted to order. But when our turn came, we were turned away. The servers refused to serve us.

This was three years before the first Green Book was published, and our humiliation was a perfect example of why such a publication was necessary. More and more people had begun to travel, but during an era of Jim Crow segregation and open discrimination, Black motorists could never be certain of the services available to them. They couldn't even be sure they would be allowed to travel in safety. The Green Book helped fill that void in information by identifying places that would welcome people of color.[12] We had no such guide in 1933, however, when we found ourselves hungry nearly five hundred miles from home.

12   Jeff Wallenfeldt, "The Green Book," Britannica.com (April 19, 2023), https://www. britannica.com/topic/The-Green-Book-travel-guide.

We had had a full day. The pride we had felt at Henry's graduation now forgotten, all we wanted was to get something to eat. And we had no idea where to get it in this alien land. I don't believe my father even asked anywhere else. We just turned toward home, angry, disappointed, and still hungry. Eventually, I quieted my bottomless adolescent stomach enough to fall asleep in the car. I am sure this was why we did not venture far from home very often, and the lesson stayed with me. I never took my own family anywhere until I had made sure we would be accommodated.

A couple of years after our trip east, I got a job as a porter in a barbershop working after school and on Saturdays. This barbershop sold all kinds of magazines, and I had plenty of opportunity to read them. There were, among others, magazines with stories about flying in World War I: *Flying Aces, G-8 and His Battle Aces*, and *Bill Barnes*, to name just three. I read them cover to cover every month when they came out, all for free.

Bill Barnes, you see, had a transport plane, and inside it was a little fighter plane. They could lower the fighter out of the airplane in midair, extend the wings, unhook it, and it could be flown around for scouting expeditions. Afterward, it would come back, get hooked up, and they'd pull the fighter back into the transport plane. These stories fanned the spark ignited in me by my first airplane ride. Now I became seriously interested in flying. A guy by the name of Scotty, another character I read about, was a hotshot pilot. I thought, *I want to be a hotshot pilot.*

In junior high school I had tried out for basketball and football. I sewed pads onto a pair of knickers to use as "football pants" even though I had to make do without shoulder pads, but none of that mattered anyway. Standing less than five feet tall and weighing maybe one hundred pounds, I was too small to make the teams.

My older brothers were two- and three-letter athletes. Henry lettered in track and football; Clarence in track, football, and basketball. By the time I got to high school in 1932, Coach Dalzell must have expected me to shoot up six inches and add thirty pounds over a summer to become a football player like my brothers. Mr. Wilbur Dalzell, the most liberal man I ever knew, was like that. He believed in you. But my body disappointed him: it didn't grow. Not to worry, though; there were competitors my size on the wrestling team, so the coach let me try out for that. Unfortunately, for all my trying, wrestling didn't work out either.

Henry had introduced me to tennis and shooting. He took me fishing upriver after I learned to swim. And I could run. Sometimes I raced the city bus to school. The bus stop was across the street from my house. If I was late, I took off running uphill and across yards and side streets and downhill and uphill, two miles plus, to the back of the school. Sometimes the bus won; sometimes I did. And if I caught the bus and didn't have to race it, I had time to buy breakfast at the store across the street from school. My breakfast was a "mild and mellow" Hershey bar, my shot of caffeine for the day. At any rate, I was halfway athletic, but the chance to distinguish myself in organized sports eluded me.

Fortunately, the position of student manager was there for the taking, and I jumped at the chance. I was good at that job. I put out and gathered up the balls for practice, packed the balls for games at home and away, sold towels for showers, helped prepare men's feet and ankles for bandaging before games (the coach was very safety-minded), changed cleats when necessary, of course ran out to supply water during games, and probably did a few other things I've forgotten. But the school principal threatened several times to have me removed from my position because of my persistent tardiness. In the end, he made good on that threat, but not before I had earned my high school letter as a student manager.

In Iowa, we skated on frozen rinks outside in the winter; Dubuque did not even have a roller-skating rink. I knew how to ice skate, and I was actually a pretty good self-taught skier. I had been ski jumping in the park across the street from my house for years; we had an ideal slope for the run-in. My friends and I would ski across the street, take off over the curb, and land on a gentle downslope. It was great fun for the kids in the neighborhood. Of course, we didn't have the proper equipment, such as ski boots. We added straps through the slots in the skis, over and around our shoes, and this improvisation kept the skis from falling off.

When I was about twelve years old, I entered the Dubuque City Junior Ski Jumping Tournament, which was organized by a group of people of Northern European descent with a love of winter sports. One boy jumped fifteen feet, but he fell. I jumped twelve feet and remained on my feet, so I was judged the winner. My award was a flashlight.

With my skis, Ames, 1941.

The experience gave me lifelong friendships with members of the Dubuque Ski Club. Mr. Ernest Keller, of Swiss descent, drove us to various cities in southern Wisconsin—places such as New Glarus, Prairie du Chien, and Madison—to enter meets sponsored by the US Ski Association. I was billed as "the only Black ski jumper in the world," which stroked my ego, but I wish I had been a better jumper. I just did not receive any training.

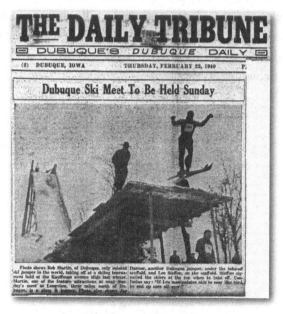

That's me, taking off.

During the winter of 1940–41, another member of the ski club, Mr. Steffen, convinced me to come home from college to jump in a local ski meet. I knew better than to do it, because I'd had no practice; I would have to just go and jump. But a college friend offered to drive me home in his car, so I went along with the plan. The day of the meet, the crosswind was quite a bit stronger than I had ever encountered. I jumped eighty-seven feet but was thrown off balance by the wind. I fell, dislocated my left shoulder, and bruised my left knee.

The next time I tried jumping was in 1945, after I had returned home from the war. I was preparing for a big meet in Cary, Illinois, way out of my class, and again, I had had no practice. I completed two practice jumps not stretching for distance. On my third jump, I tried for a better distance, jumped too far, and landed hard on an almost level slope. My body was shocked. The next morning I awoke to find myself paralyzed; I could move only my hands and wrists. Using them, I worked my body to the edge of the bed until my feet swung down and I sat up. I did recover, but this time I listened to my inner voice and my body. Trying to ski jump without proper conditioning and practice was foolhardy. I could have died—after returning safely from the war! Once I realized that, my ski jumping career was over.

There were, of course, still more things to try. At the age of seventeen, I decided I had to own a bicycle. My father didn't think it was a good idea. He said bicycles were too dangerous on the hilly streets of Dubuque. But my job as a porter meant that I had my own money, and the local service station had bikes. After I'd arranged to pay fifty cents per week, I took home a fifty-dollar Schwinn bicycle.

✪» Capt. Robert L. Martin

By the second day of riding, I didn't think I needed handlebars. I was riding down a hill at about thirty-five miles per hour when I swerved to miss a mound in the pavement. Suddenly, the bicycle was riding me. I slid on my stomach and arms for about one hundred yards on the brick washboard pavement, but somehow the handlebars got around me, and the bike was not damaged too much. More important, of course, was my safety. Auto traffic happened to be light—a fact that probably saved my life. I dragged myself and the bike to the curb.

A woman came along and asked, "Are you hurt?"

No, I wasn't badly hurt—except for my ego. I could recover from the bruises on my arms and knees. I got back on my bicycle and rode to work. After that, my father decided to help pay for the bike—maybe because I had learned to use the handlebars.

I got along well with people, but a lot of what I did, I did alone. By high school, most of the boys I had hung out with were mixing socially with the girls a little, but somehow I was not included. Girls seemed to come into these guys' lives, but none of them took me into their circle. I was pretty much on my own, being the only Black kid in my class all the way up through high school and college.

I had had friends before high school. I went to Charlie's house once in a while with a couple of other guys in the neighborhood. At one point, Jimmy invited me into his house. He lived up the block in one of the very fine wooden homes. His father owned the local drugstore. Jimmy invited me up into his attic to see his electric train. Nothing was broken while I was there, and we didn't investigate any of the rooms of his home. We just went up to the attic and played with the train. Even so, he must have been reproached by his parents, because he never invited me in again.

All through junior high and high school, one of the highlights of the spring semester was a ride on a big amusement boat that would come up the river. Students paid to get on, both boys and girls, with the girls' mothers very much in evidence. The boat left around ten in the morning and came back around three thirty in the afternoon, so we brought our lunches along. The trip was somewhat like going to an amusement park, with coin slot games where you could lose your money.

There was also a band, a Black band, that played dance music. I had no one to dance with—and in fact didn't even know how to dance with someone—but I would spend hours listening to the music; I got a kick out of watching the band play. I also watched the water, the big paddlewheel, and the shore. It was always an interesting day, but I did feel somewhat isolated. I knew there were groups. I just was not invited into any.

I have always loved music, and have always enjoyed singing, dancing, and playing music on the radio. I did have a few violin and piano lessons when I was young, but I didn't practice or go regularly to lessons. I never played a composition. I just did not like music lessons. About the time I was supposed to start learning the scales, somebody realized that I was not going to be a pianist or violinist, and the lessons stopped—but not the music.

The songs I heard on the radio were the ones being played in Chicago at the Aragon and the Trianon ballrooms. The Trianon was on the South Side of Chicago. One side of it faced the Black community, yet it was closed to us until much later, shortly before it closed for good. I knew the songs that were played there. I heard the music and learned the words, but I didn't go to any dances in Dubuque, because there was nobody I could go with except my sister.

Once or twice every year, generally on a Sunday, my father would take the family and drive to Chicago. I helped with the driving as soon as I was old enough. We would leave Dubuque around four in the morning, arriving around 10:00 a.m. We came for White Sox and Cubs ball games, but we preferred the White Sox games because we thought they played against better ball clubs, like the Yankees. After the games, we got together with friends that my father had known before moving north. We would have dinner at their house and play parlor games in the afternoon. There were no Blacks in Dubuque for us to socialize with, so meeting friends in Chicago was a lot of fun for us. Once in a great while, we would go to an amusement park farther north, called Riverview. White City Amusement Park was closer, at Sixty-Third and what is now King Drive, but Black people could go there only on certain days, and we didn't go to Chicago to visit White City Amusement Park anyway. After our visit with Dad's friends, we would drive home the same evening so my father could open his office at nine the next morning.

While I was still in high school, Hettie went off to chiropody college in Chicago. Newsstands there offered song sheets with the words to all the music that was currently being played on the radio, and whenever we came to Chicago, I made sure to get my hands on them. But these were not the songs that Hettie danced to at parties on south Forty-Seventh Street, where Black people played music and held dances. Their songs could not be found on printed sheets. I learned them from the friends we came to see in Chicago.

After high school graduation in 1936, I evaluated my choices. I could help my father in his chiropody office or, better yet, follow in the family business and study chiropody as Clarence and Hettie had done before me. Unfortunately, working with feet just did not appeal to me. I could also continue working as a barbershop porter until it was my turn to go to college. I could earn ten dollars each week shining shoes, another two dollars cleaning the shop and providing water, and a dollar fifty for mopping the National Tea Company store next door one night a week. So that's what I did.

When the fall of 1938 finally rolled around, I had my chance to attend college. I went away to what was then officially known as Iowa State College of Agricultural and Mechanic Arts in Ames—Iowa State, for short. I was excited to attend classes there, but I could not live on campus; the dorms were closed to me. So was the YMCA. During my first quarter, I stayed at the home of a local family with the last name of Martin, who were of no relation to me. Other Black male students stayed there as well. Black girls lived at the home of the Ship family while they attended college at Ames. We students ate with our host family, and we socialized a little. But there were no other Black engineering students at Iowa State at the time, and in fact, except for one guy in my ROTC class, there were no other Black students in any of my classes there. My college social life was similar to what I had experienced in high school.

I took two years of ROTC training, by the way, but was not allowed to take the two years of advanced classes that would have earned me an officer's commission. I did not get to take a sharpshooting class. As I told Tom Fruehling of the local *Gazette* years later, "No matter which way a Black man turned, there was always something holding him back. I learned lessons in independence."[13]

We Black college students did not go to the homecoming festivities on campus either. We had our separate homecoming dance that was not

---

[13]   Tom Fruehling, "Lessons in Independence," the *Gazette*, July 2, 2000.

sponsored by the college, although most who attended were students there. We rented the ballroom in the city park. Our dance music was played on records. These records had all the latest Afro-American hits as well as all the "regular" popular hits. Our banquet consisted of picnic food: hot dogs, baked beans, and the like.

In a student enrollment of about six thousand at Iowa State at the time, there were, I think, about twenty Black students, and that's about how many came to our homecoming dance. There were a few "part-time" students too, who did not have the money they needed to stay in school continuously. They would drop out of school, work for a semester, then go back to school. I liked a girl from Des Moines, but we never had more than just a friendship.

Staying with the Martin family worked out fine, but I did not like hitchhiking to school. People were quite willing to pick up any student and give them a lift to "Dogtown," as they called it, the campus area, which was about a mile from the city proper. I just did not like having to wait for a ride. So, after my first quarter, I found a place to stay at the home of the Madison family, who lived closer to campus.

Finally, I found an apartment in Dogtown, right across the street from the college, and I chose to move out there. I lived there for the rest of my college career, either two or three years, and had a roommate at least part of the time. Louis Green was a graduate student who had studied under George Washington Carver at Tuskegee; he did not share any of my classes. The apartment I shared with him was close to a restaurant that had no problem serving me. For breakfast I could get a roll and a cup of coffee if I had time before class.

I tried out for the football team at Iowa State during my first semester even though I knew full well I would not make it onto the team. Iowa State did not allow Black athletes on their teams while I was a student there. This school played in the Big Six Conference along with Missouri, Oklahoma, Kansas, Kansas State, and Nebraska, and there was an implied threat that Black athletes might get hurt. This was because of the experience of Jack Trice, who played for Iowa State in 1923. He was the first Black athlete at the school and the only one at the time in the entire Big Six.

Jack was expected to do great things for his team. His first real college game was played against the University of Minnesota in Minneapolis. He reportedly stayed in the same hotel as his teammates, but he was not allowed to join them in the dining room. This seemed to have little effect on Jack, though, because he was completely focused on the game. He was prepared to give his all, not knowing this would actually mean his life.

In the second play of the game, Jack suffered a broken collarbone but kept on playing. In the third quarter, he was trampled by several Minnesota players. He still wanted to keep playing, but when he could not even stand up, he was sent to the hospital. The next day, doctors decided that Jack was fit to travel. He rode home with his teammates only to die of internal injuries two days later.

Was Jack Trice specifically targeted for injury because of his race? No one can say for sure, but Iowa State did not play against Minnesota again for sixty-six years.[14]

Much better, and better connected, Black athletes than I had passed up the opportunity to study at Iowa State because they knew they would not be allowed to play. But I knew it was time for the school to stop "protecting" us by denying us access. Nothing would change unless someone stepped up to challenge the status quo, so I volunteered as that challenger. Even doing this, I knew that the coaches at Iowa State were not the only barriers. Missouri and Oklahoma would definitely refuse to play against me, but I thought there might be a possibility of playing in Kansas or Nebraska. I just hoped that my presence might help break down the barrier one day.

Mind you, I didn't go back to Coach Dalzell and ask him if I should do this. That would have been silly. He did not advise kids weighing 120 pounds to go out for football. But I was willing to learn the game. I got out there and, right away, got my shoulder dislocated while trying to stop somebody. The guy just took my arm right with him. One of the assistant coaches set my arm back in place, so I think I finished that scrimmage. Then, a couple of days later, I got that arm knocked out of place again. That was it. I could see where this was going, so I quit football and went on with my education. A few years later, another Black fellow did the same thing with the same result. He couldn't make the team either, even though he had been a star player in high school. The world was not yet ready for us.

---

[14]   Dorothy Schwieder, "The Life and Legacy of Jack Trice," *The Annals of Iowa* 69, no. 4 (Fall 2010), https://history.iowa.gov/history/education/educator-resources/primary-source-sets/iowa-leader-civil-rights-and-equality/life.

During my junior year in college, the US government announced the Civilian Pilot Training Program. Here was a chance to learn to fly for about fifty dollars: twenty-five dollars for the course and twenty-five dollars for the physical examination.

My father was quite progressive. He said, "Sure, go ahead and take this course. Learn to fly."

Maybe my father remembered my declaration more than six years earlier that I would become a pilot. Maybe he realized that flying, unlike football, was something ideally suited to my size. Anyway, I paid the fee and submitted my application. It had to get clearance from Washington.

I was told, essentially, "You've got to hold a minute on this course before we can okay it, but you go ahead and assume you're going to get in. If anything happens, we'll let you know."

The Civilian Pilot Training Program, or CPTP, taught more than four hundred thirty-five thousand people to fly, including hundreds of women and around two thousand Black men. Begun by the government in 1939 with the potential for national defense and largely phased out by the summer of 1944, at its peak it involved more than fourteen hundred flight schools and eleven hundred educational institutions. The program included six Black colleges, but in various places across the country where an individual Black person would sign up, local mores took over.[15] Some places would say yes, he could take the course, which included college credit; others would say no, he could not. Anyway, the training had to be cleared through Washington, and luckily, Washington okayed mine. There were no other Black students in this course; James Bowman from Des Moines came to the program a little after my time there, but I did not know about him until later.

I began civilian flight training in February of 1941. My first solo flight was in April, in a civilian-type monoplane, a high-wing Luscomb with side-by-side seating. My training continued through that summer and finished in August. I earned my private pilot's license three months before the attack on Pearl Harbor.

---

15   Cassie Peterson, "The History of the Civilian Pilot Training Program: Preparing Future WW2 Pilots on a Massive Scale," *Plane and Pilot Magazine*, June 3, 2022, https://www.planeandpilotmag.com/news/pilot-talk/the-history-of-the-civilian-pilot-training-program/.

As expected, I loved flying. This engineering student took naturally to the study needed for accurate and safe navigation in the air. I worked hard to perfect my technique, challenged myself to get ever better at my craft. At Tuskegee, I made notes in my pilot's log about what had worked well and what had not, such as "sleepy, hot landing," "22,000 ft. sloppy formation," and "good to bad, better." In another note, I remarked that "Draper [my primary flight instructor] said he was pleased," but that I thought I was "flying lousy." Even during civilian flight training at Iowa State, I held myself to my own standard of excellence. In return, my level of competence, together with quick thinking, may well have saved my life more than once.

While I was still completing my civilian training in the Luscomb, I flew up to practice stalls and spins. I pulled up into a stall, and the propeller stopped straight up, right in front of me, just as expected. Now I had to dive so that the engine would start and run the way it had when the instructor was in the plane with me. Only this time it did not. I dived the plane. The propeller spun beautifully, but the engine would not start. After a couple of tries, I gave up and looked for a place to land.

There was a very large pasture in sight, and I set up my landing pattern with an approach into the wind. I slowed the plane's airspeed by sideslipping and leveled off to land. The plane floated and floated and floated across the pasture. At the far side of the field, the plane and I came to a fence. I prayed something and jerked back on the stick. The plane made it over the fence and plopped into a muddy cornfield three-point dead, meaning it dropped down on all three wheels at once and just stopped. I was only ten feet beyond the fence.

I got out, surveyed the situation, and decided to fly out. Using my belt, I tied the stick back. I hoped I had set the brakes and that they would hold. Then I primed the engine, got out again, and pulled the prop through just as I had done when starting out at the airfield. The engine caught and ran. The brakes held.

I climbed into the plane, gunned the engine, and started rolling in the muddy cornfield. I carefully nursed the plane up to flying speed while keeping it from nosing over, and I took off. I flew back to the airfield, landed, and told my story. That's when I learned that while I was starting the plane, other planes from the airfield were flying overhead, watching me and trying to signal me not to try to take off. It was too dangerous! But I did not get the message.

There were four ways I could have been killed in this deadstick landing. The plane could have hit the fence, flipped, and killed me in the wreckage. The prop could have hit me while I was starting the engine. The plane could have moved forward or turned, and the prop would have chewed me up then. Or the plane could have nosed over in the muddy field as I tried to fly out and trapped me in the fire. But none of those things happened. Even then I did have some idea of what I was doing—and maybe a little luck. Anyway, I lived to tell the tale.

The war was already going on in Europe and Africa, and America was helping the Allies as much as possible without formally declaring war. Young men at college were missing class roll calls if their last names ended with -off, -owski, or if they had any other very common European surname. These guys were eager to fight. Men in the active reserve program wore their uniforms to class and seriously asked the rest of us, "When are you gonna join up?" Never, I hoped. I still had another year of college to finish.

I did not want to go to war … Oh, yes, I did … Oh, no, I didn't. But the yeas outweighed the nays. I had volunteered for flying on the cheap, on the war department's dime. They let me finish school without drafting me. I decided I would volunteer to go into the air corps, not knowing that the air corps was only now becoming a possibility for me. Truth be told, with mustered bravado I ate it up, the idea of gold bars and silver wings. Yes, I wanted to walk the world wearing the silver wings of a pilot and the bars of a commissioned officer. Here I was at the top of life. I hadn't had a loaded gun pointed at me, hadn't seen a dead body, but I was ready to leap into that unknown. *Do your part, hero; win the war! And don't get killed.*

CHAPTER 3

I WANTED A FIGHTER

I graduated with my electrical engineering degree from Iowa State in June of 1942 and immediately began applying for jobs. The school had invited big manufacturing companies to interview graduating seniors and, potentially, offer them jobs. I don't remember even talking to any of them. Many, if not most, of my classmates had job offers by the time they graduated. Probably half had government work studying radar, but I was not interested in that. I wanted to work with power and illumination, and even months after graduation, all I had for my effort was a stack of rejection letters. I could not get a job anywhere. Maybe it wasn't just aeronautical engineering jobs that were closed to me; maybe the world wasn't ready for a Black electrical engineer either.

As it turned out, my career had to wait anyway. Uncle Sam had been good enough to bide his time until after I had graduated, but the war was on, and I knew he wouldn't wait much longer. I went to the draft board in Des Moines and told them that I wanted to volunteer for the air corps, which at that time was part of the army. There I sat in the same room as other potential cadets, all of them white. We took the exam together and then waited until proctors called out our scores.

When my score was announced, I could see the other applicants' surprise that I had done so well. But why wouldn't I? I was a college graduate with an electrical engineering degree. And unlike many of them, I already had some flying experience. I scored a very high mark, and the board told me to go home and wait for a call or a letter telling me where to report. I returned to Dubuque to await further instructions.

Meanwhile, the draft boards were trying to meet their quotas of black bodies and white bodies, and I did not yet have my orders for the air corps. I received a letter from the draft board of Story County, where Ames is located, instructing me to report.

I called them from my home in Dubuque and said, "I volunteered for the air corps. I passed the examination. My papers are in Washington, so I don't think I need to be drafted."

The draft board responded with something like "Well, buddy, you are drafted. You'd better be here or we're sending MPs after you."

I reported. I went to the army induction center, repeated my story, and showed them my papers. The army instructed me to wait there. I was in the army anyway, whether or not I was actually accepted into the air corps, so all I had to do was follow orders. I stayed at the induction center until the army told me I should report to Camp Dodge. On September 5, 1942, I entered the service in Company B, Camp Dodge, Iowa. I would remain there as a supply room clerk for seven months.

My dad came to visit me when I was first inducted into the army. Fall 1942.

In Dubuque with my sisters Hettie (left), Vivian, and Lillian (right).

Dad with his sisters, Rosetta (left) and Lelia.

The little company I joined was responsible for getting new recruits into uniform and accompanying them to the train so they could go wherever they were assigned. It had a couple of barracks to house the two or three hundred men who would come in at a time. During their brief stay there, the men got their shots and got fitted with clothing, and to make that happen, somebody had to handle the boxes of work uniforms in the warehouse. That was my job while I stayed there, something the inductees didn't have to get pulled out of the ranks to do. After a day or so, once outfitted, the men would be lined up, told where they were going, and put on a train. Then away they went, to be replaced by another batch of recruits.

I was just a spare private assigned to help the supply sergeant so I would have a job. I was having a good time. Nobody was shooting at me, and I wasn't doing any training. Of course, the army was segregated in Des Moines, as it was anywhere else at that time, but maybe the segregation was a little less rigid than elsewhere. Camp Dodge, where only Black inductees were sent, was on the north side of Des Moines. Fort Des Moines, where the white inductees went, was on the south side. The Women's Army Corps (WAC), also trained on the south side. White and Black WACs trained separately but on the same base. Soldiers could come from Camp Dodge to the open-house events and dances held on Friday nights at the small, segregated United Service Organization (USO) post in Des Moines. For me, these were days of wine and roses.

The fact that I wanted to enter the air corps didn't mean anything to the army personnel to whom I showed my papers, but the papers that came back from Washington told them I would be assigned to the air corps. These papers stated that I should be held at the induction center until Washington found a place for me in the pilot training program.

I had dreams of going to Scott Field in Illinois or Randolph Field in Texas, or any of the other fine training fields. I couldn't imagine that there would be a segregated Black squadron with its own airfield, its own training, its own support staff—everything. The prejudice I had experienced in Iowa, where all my classmates were white, was nothing compared to the great umbrella of prejudice that covered everything in the military. Here, Blacks were assigned their own little corner of whatever area of the service they entered. I thought I would learn flying along with a thousand other aviation cadets at some big field in Texas. Nope. The day came, and the orders were "Martin, you are going to Tuskegee."

I was only dimly aware of all the obstacles that had to be eliminated before I was allowed to fly at all. I had gone through college, had received a bachelor of science degree in electrical engineering, and had earned college credits alongside white classmates. My acceptance into the civilian flying training program had had to come from Washington, but in Iowa we didn't know everything that was happening elsewhere. The army and the navy fought against letting Black soldiers into the higher service ranks. They admitted Blacks into officer training school only if forced, as I should have recognized from my brother's experience.

Henry, ten years older than I, had enlisted in the navy. He was top man in his navy class, so he asked to go to quartermaster school. Well, the quartermaster in the navy is the man who runs the ship. The captain is up there, but the quartermaster runs the ship. They told him no. But since he had a degree in chemical engineering, they sent him to work at a navy lab on Staten Island. There, he was testing oil one day and discovered that there were impurities in it that wouldn't ordinarily be there. It had been sabotaged. He reported this and, as a reward, finally received a recommendation for officer candidate school (OCS). When Henry graduated, he was only the fiftieth Black soldier ever to be commissioned as an officer in the US Navy. I was approximately the three hundredth in the air corps, in a class of twenty-five after the previous 285 graduates. We were one of a very few Black families at the time, if not the only, with two officers in different branches of the military at the same time.

Me, a first lieutenant, and my brother
Henry Martin, a lieutenant (junior grade).

As an ensign in the US Navy, Henry A. Martin went to Osaka, Japan, after the war, not in charge of a ship but in charge of a company that did stevedore work, loading and unloading ships. The requirements of segregation thwarted my brother's ambitions just as they had threatened Benjamin Davis's career.

I was transferred to the corps of aviation cadets, Tuskegee Army Air Force, Tuskegee, Alabama, on April 25, 1943, seven months after I had arrived at Camp Dodge. The army sent me to Tuskegee via Pullman. I didn't have any trouble getting onto the train at the station in Des Moines. I was in uniform, and a few marines and army guys on the train were also in uniform. During most of the trip, we played cards together—no big money. We went to sleep in a regular Pullman berth and woke up in New Orleans. That's when things were a bit different.

When I arrived at the dining car for breakfast that morning, I was ushered to a section away from the other guests. A curtain was pulled closed to separate me from the white folks dining there. I was surprised to find myself singled out to dine alone, but it didn't take much reflection to know why. I had known things were different in the South. I also knew that protesting would do no good and would only serve to poison my own attitude. I resolved that no insult could bother me. After all, I was going to train for the army air corps!

Although my army ticket called for a Pullman all the way to Montgomery, Alabama, it was explained to me in New Orleans that I would not ride that way for the rest of my trip. A priest in the depot, acting as an ombudsman for troops going through, pulled me aside and informed me that railroads always attached "hollis" in parentheses after a Black person's name on the Pullman reservation list. Anywhere down the line, the next agent knew who was coming and could void the reservation. I could get a Pullman only if there happened to be enough other Black passengers to fill the entire car, and of course Uncle Sam would not wait for me while I waited for fellow travelers. I had no choice but to ride the remaining 350 miles of my trip in the coach section.

Someone else who had traveled in the South informed me that when I got to Tuskegee, I could turn in my ticket to the finance office and they would refund the difference between the cost of the first-class Pullman and the coach seating I had been forced to take—a small consolation for the insult and inconvenience I had had to bear through no fault of mine! The same thing happened again in 1945, by the way, when I was traveling from a rest camp in California to the base at Tuskegee. Beyond New Orleans, no Pullman was available even for a war veteran. I should have been protected from discrimination by federal law governing interstate travel, but I was not.

The deeply oppressive prejudice common in the Deep South at that time should have caused someone to hesitate before placing a Black army air corps training program there. The local population was formally opposed to the entire plan. Tuskegee Institute was, however, a well-known Black college that already had an established aviation program. In addition, the town had a hospital for Black people.[16] Maybe those in charge assumed that Black pilots would crash planes daily and need a lot of medical assistance. Of course we did not crash any more frequently than anyone else, but elsewhere, an ill or injured Black man might have had to wait at the end of a line and die waiting. Besides, Tuskegee had weather that allowed year-round flying. Our comfort in the surrounding community was hardly the army's first consideration anyway. Tuskegee was where we were placed.

Instead of initially allowing Black cadets to choose specialties such as navigation or bombardment, which would have required racially integrated training, the air corps decided to start us off with pursuit flying. Pursuit flying required a single pilot to learn flying, navigation, and gunnery skills all together, making it the most dangerous form of combat flying and the most difficult to learn. It was, however, the cheapest option for a self-contained unit.

The levels of difficulty and danger posed by the new program must have seemed irrelevant to those who thought no Black applicant would qualify for the program anyway. Air corps administrators did not expect us to pass the new Army General Classification Test (AGCT) in the highest category, as needed. The AGCT was biased toward those with more education, and this was layered on top of the already stringent requirements of the air corps. Imagine administrators' surprise when far more Black candidates

---

[16]   This was the site of the infamous Tuskegee experiment, conducted between 1932 and 1972, that studied the effects of syphilis in 399 Black men. These men believed they were being treated for syphilis when in fact they were not, even after penicillin became available for treatment. Centers for Disease Control and Prevention, "The Syphilis Study at Tuskegee Timeline," *The U.S. Public Health Service Syphilis Study at Tuskegee*, Dec. 5, 2022, https://www.cdc.gov/tuskegee/timeline.htm.

qualified for the program than their quota allowed! However, in spite of deep prejudice within the military leadership as well as the surrounding community, and in spite of what seemed to be built-in mechanisms for failure, the pilot training program for Blacks was indeed designed to produce good pilots, just in case some of us made it through. This was largely due to the influence of Dr. Lewis A. Jackson, our first director of training; Colonel Noel Parrish, the fair-minded commander of Tuskegee Army Airfield; and General Benjamin Davis, Sr., from inside the War Department. Quality training gave us the real opportunity we needed.

The 99th Pursuit Squadron was activated on March 21, 1941, and the thirteen flying cadets selected for the first class, only five of whom would graduate, began training at Tuskegee on July 19 of that year.[17] On April 19, First Lady Eleanor Roosevelt, a trustee of Tuskegee Institute, had asked about the civilian flying school when she was on campus to tour a clinic there. She wanted to meet its director, Charles Alfred "Chief" Anderson.

As Anderson recalls, during their conversation, Mrs. Roosevelt asked him, "Can Negroes really fly airplanes?"

He replied, "Certainly we can! We fly every day down here; as a matter of fact, would you like to take an airplane ride?"

Mrs. Roosevelt's Secret Service contingent panicked when she accepted, but she would not be dissuaded. After her thirty-minute ride, she turned to Anderson and remarked, "I guess Negroes can fly."[18]

Her much-publicized flight with him had certainly put that question to rest. It was also a public relations boost for the new program, which was supposed to determine whether Black pilots could be trained for military service.

At first, a Tuskegee pilot was required to be a college graduate. But education does not protect anyone from getting killed; a guy with a college degree is just as vulnerable as anyone else. Eventually, the requirement was relaxed to two years of college training, and then whatever training the pilot had was acceptable as long as he could pass the examination.

If a guy had some God-given sense and ordinary education, he didn't need a degree to learn how to operate an airplane. Without a college

---

[17] Charles E. Francis, *Tuskegee Airmen: The Men Who Changed a Nation* (Boston: Brandon Books, 2008), 51.

[18] Francis, *Tuskegee Airmen*, 398

degree, a pilot served as a warrant officer. He performed the same job as a commissioned officer, just without salutes from enlisted personnel. Later in the war, I understand, the college education requirement for pilots was reinstated just in case some would go up the military officer grade scale. But during the war, we pilots really were just flying guns.

Even with relaxed wartime recruitment standards, the system by which we cadets were allowed to continue our training was extremely selective. From preflight all the way through, we were under constant observation. They had checked our record of scholastic achievement; now they measured our flying ability. There were twenty-, forty-, and sixty-hour checks at all levels: primary, basic, and advanced flight training. This was standard procedure for all pilots, to make sure we had mastered certain levels of ability after so many hours.

In addition, the program itself had very strict protocols like those at West Point. For instance, the only time we walked was in formation; we ran at double time if we went anywhere alone. Most Black cadets had never heard of this high level of restriction and regimentation. After all, we had no role models; Black military officers were almost nonexistent at that time.

Beyond flight checks and military protocols, however, more than exacting standards were at work in the selection process. At Tuskegee, any mistake could get a man eliminated, or not. It was arbitrary. He could be eliminated for his inability to fly, but also for rules infractions or too many demerits: tie untied, shirt unbuttoned, shoes left dusty, bed not made properly. He could be washed out because of his attitude or because his instructor did not like him or just didn't feel good that day. White officers used the quota system any way they wanted; only a certain number of cadets per class were allowed to graduate. The washout rate at Tuskegee was 58 percent compared to 41 percent for white flying cadets.

I knew a guy who was eliminated on graduation day. He had been measured for his officer's uniform like all the rest of us. His shirt and trouser size were recorded, and when the uniforms came, he tried his on and hung it up just like everyone else to wait for graduation day.

On that day, the formation was marching to the graduation ceremony when a white officer standing on the headquarters veranda said, "Stop that formation. There's one too many men in it." So the formation was ordered to halt.

They went inside, checked the records, came out and said to Edward Flowers, "You, get out of the formation and come inside," which he did while the rest of the formation went on. This was just about noon.

They told him, "You are not going to graduate."

No reason was given, or at least he didn't tell me what reason they gave him. They took away his officer's clothes, put him back in enlisted men's clothing, packed him up, and shipped him away. At two thirty that afternoon, he was headed for Florida. He did not fly anymore. He had made it all the way through the training, yet through no fault of his, he was not allowed to graduate.

Maybe Eddie took it philosophically. Maybe he told himself, "So they kicked me out; I'm okay." But I really think it bothered him for the rest of his life. We were not in the same class, but I moved into his neighborhood in Chicago after the war. I lived four doors away from him on Forty-Ninth Street, and when I ran into him, he was drinking heavily. Every afternoon, he came home from work and just drank. Finally, I guess his liver quit working and he died.

I wish Eddie Flowers had stayed around long enough to see his wife in later years. He would have been proud, I think. She finally decided that if she were ever going to make a parachute jump, she'd better just do it. She planned the trip with my daughter, and they both jumped with the Golden Eagles. I'm proud that my daughter had the courage to do that, but Eddie Flowers's wife? She was ninety years old when she jumped out of that airplane.

I entered the flight training program at Tuskegee in April, 1943, just after the 99th had shipped out. Our class, 44-A, so named because we would be the first class to graduate in 1944, came from many parts of the country. One guy was from Pocatello, Idaho. Clarence Driver was from Los Angeles, and there were guys from New York and Omaha. Frank Roberts was from Boston; Sanford Perkins, from Denver; Alexander Jefferson and Robert O'Neil, from Michigan; Charles Jackson, from Chicago.

Since I was already in the service, unlike some cadets who came in as civilians, I went directly to the Tuskegee Army Airfield, about six miles northwest of town. I wrote my name and identifying information in the brown book we were all issued. I, Robert Leander Martin, army air forces cadet, was twenty-four years old, five feet eight inches tall, and weighed 152 pounds. Recruits were supposed to be about five feet six or five feet eight, maybe five feet ten at the most, and weigh less than 170 pounds. The cockpit of the P-39 was made for a man this size.

A fighter plane, like any airplane, is designed to carry a certain load. With the engine, wings, and surfaces, it is calculated that a particular plane will lift off the ground and fly at a certain airspeed with a certain load. The plane has to be able to fly out and return, so it has to hold a certain amount of gasoline. Engineers tailored the amount of ammunition the plane could carry—bombs, in particular—around these fixed weights plus that of a man. Ideally, the man would be in a small range, around five feet eight and 140–155 pounds. Too much weight and he was displacing needed gasoline. The plane didn't have to fit like a glove, but there was not much room to play with.

Despite these stated size limits for fighter pilots, politics and politicians could always get certain people into the program who did not meet these requirements. Some entered and got their wings and commission when they were over six feet tall and weighed two hundred pounds. One way to lift with a greater load was to stay on the ground longer to build up greater airspeed, but that was the pilot's problem to solve.

The training program was set up this way: When a cadet entered the Sixty-sixth flying training detachment, the unit governing all the flying training at Tuskegee, he went into preflight classes. There were four and a half weeks in lower preflight and four and a half weeks in upper preflight. This was followed by nine weeks each of primary, basic, and advanced flight training. Each level was split into lower and upper sections of four and a half weeks each. Finally, if we made it all the way through this eight-month process, we were ready to graduate and go on to transition flight training.

Preflight began for me on May 2, 1943, and was conducted on the base. Here we had ground school, where we learned about flying, the airplane we would fly, and meteorology. We also drilled, marched, participated in athletics, and learned the army way of life and its many regulations, but there was no basic training. They left that for the infantry. Our marching drill was no worse than it was in the rest of the army, and there were no fourteen- or twenty-mile hikes. We had no packs, no rifle drills. We learned about guns but weren't issued a weapon; we would not use a weapon until we could fly the airplane and become a flying gun.

After the successful completion of nine weeks of preflight training at the army airfield, we were transferred to Tuskegee Institute, in the heart of town, where we began primary flight training. We were housed in institute buildings and given instruction in institute classrooms, but these were not normal college classes. They were strictly air corps flight training classes, taught by special Black instructors. We did not mingle with the student body enrolled at Tuskegee Institute. We were *at* the Institute but not a *part* of it.

Like preflight training, the primary phase was nine weeks long. We logged sixty hours of training at Moton Field, on the northeast corner of town. Here, there were two large brick hangars and grass, not paved, runways. A bus brought us to the field and took us back to campus after each flying session. The lower primary class always flew in the morning, the upper class in the afternoon. The daily routine concluded with an evening ceremony, retreat, and mess in our own dining room.

Moton Field was the only primary flight facility for Black cadets in the army air corps. Back in Iowa, the majority of the population was white, and they ran everything. Here in the primary flight program, the population was Black, so Blacks ran everything. There were white test pilots who checked the students for proficiency and advanced the ones who had completed the training. If a person was washed out, that was done by white officers; they had control over who graduated and who did not. But the instructors in the primary program were all Black civilians. And even in the midst of a racist culture, surrounded by a hostile town, it worked because we were not thrust into the general population.

The town of Tuskegee was the only place, except the Chehaw train station, where we encountered the local white populace. These people definitely wore their prejudice on their sleeves. I went into town a couple of times but saw nothing worth buying in the stores, so I didn't feel the need to keep returning there. Classes and flying kept me busy. I didn't have time to go looking for trouble. My family upbringing had conditioned me to avoid anything that could have reflected poorly on my father's business, and now I had every incentive to avoid trouble so I would not be washed out. I kept my distance. That included avoiding the movie theater in town.

When I was growing up in Dubuque, there was an upper balcony in one theater, but Black people did not have to go up there. Times had changed a little by then in some places. We could see movies on the main floor. At the regular movie house in Tuskegee, however, we were required to go around to the side and climb up really high, to what was called "nigger heaven" at the time, to see a movie. There was also the option of going to another town for recreation if someone had leisure time, which I didn't, but a person still had to go into town to catch the bus. For me, it just was not worth it.

Yes, there was a morale problem at Tuskegee. It felt demeaning, even dangerous, to venture into town, but recreational outlets on base were scarcely better. In this hot Alabama region, there was no swimming pool available to us. The post exchange (PX) itself was poorly supplied, and of course it was segregated. We could visit the small Black-owned business section—the "block," as it was called—which was adjacent to the campus of Tuskegee Institute. We could purchase candy and ice cream in the drugstore there and ogle the coeds who happened to be parading down the street. But there was no USO club where we could relax and meet hostesses or attend Saturday-night dances.

A USO club, a decent PX, or a swimming pool certainly would have helped boost our morale, but at Tuskegee, we really had no free time. We were in an intensive training unit where they kept us busy with exercises and classes all day long. At night we were tired and went to sleep. Sometimes we flew on Sundays; sometimes we didn't. But training went on seven days a week because, we were told, the war was going on seven days a week. Really, nothing prepares you for this sort of training. You don't know what's coming up next; you just meet each day as it comes. Then, after your training, when you go over to combat, it's just another day.

In primary training, we learned the rudiments of flying—taking off, maneuvers, landing—and we got a little bit of cross-country experience. The instructors knew their business, and they were very businesslike. We could not talk to them in the air. They had to teach us to fly so well that we, they, and the entire primary flying school were above reproach. Our instructors knew that we had to learn to operate a plane in the precise manner called for in regulations because otherwise we would be eliminated—either by our white commissioned army examiner or by the white instructors we would have afterward.

I began primary flight training on July 3, 1943. The first plane I flew for the army was an open-cockpit biplane, the Stearman PT-17 Continental, which had a seven-cylinder air-cooled radial engine and 220 horsepower. According to the log I kept, my first flight was one hour, one minute long.

I don't recall meeting other cadets with previous flying experience; many had never been in a light plane before, and everything was totally new to them. My civilian pilot training must have made military instruction easier for me. I certainly was not afraid of flying. But my instructor didn't give me a pass because I already knew how to do some things; there was always more to learn. There was always something to perfect.

We needed to know how to fly under extreme conditions, so instructors yelled at cadets, stormed at them, used strong language, called them everything but a child of God—but we never heard the N word. Even the white instructors we had later on knew better than that.

There was an unwritten law that if we did hear that word, there were supposed to be two deaths at one and the same time on that day; after all, we were at the controls of an airplane and they were our passengers. We were born to die anyway. But we got through without that. There was no point in the use of such language because this training was meant to improve us, not degrade us.

Here's an exercise: when you are learning to fly, pick out two trees, one here, another there. Use a nearby road as your starting point and keep the first tree on your wing. Fly a perfect circle around this tree, then come around and fly a perfect circle around the second tree. Don't lose altitude! The goal is to wind up over the road at the same height and same position as before. That's what your instructor grades you on; that is what he has taught you to do. On my big examination day, though, there were three trees. When I came out of one circle, I lined up, found a tree on my wingtip, and flew around it. But when I returned, I had no idea whether I was flying around the same tree as before. When I got back on the ground, my instructor said, "Next time, don't pick three trees!"

My primary instructor also taught me how to fly upside down. We went up a little extra high, turned the plane over, and glided down, trying to make circles to show complete mastery of the plane. A cadet stood in awe of his instructor, Black or white. This man held all the power. There was no social connection between cadets and instructors; it just was not the thing to do.

After primary flight training, we returned to Tuskegee Army Airfield for nine weeks of basic flight training. Here we still had Black classroom instructors, but the flying instructors were white officers. I'd had no problem with white instructors before, so I did not find anything to get excited about with this change—nothing to upset my living and learning.

Internal problems between cadets were almost nonexistent. With a student body on the base composed of preflight cadets (P/C), basic cadets (B/C), and advanced cadets (A/C), there was harmony. Preflight cadets did not socialize with upperclassmen. Whenever questioned by an upperclassman, they used their loudest voice to answer, "Yes sir," "No sir," or "No excuse, sir."

Hazing was on the playful side. One of the first indoctrinations was the dodo verses. These were inane paragraphs to be shouted while standing at attention whenever requested by an upperclassman. After all, in the army we could be given any order, and we had to obey it. No upperclassman could physically touch a P/C "dummy." He could, however, order a P/C to perform exercises until both were too tired to continue. He could report a P/C for violation of regulations, giving him demerits that might call for walking punishment tours. He could not have a P/C dismissed from the training program.

We actually had a wonderful esprit de corps. Every cadet wanted every other cadet to succeed. Our enemy was not another cadet but the white power structure of the military. Since we were, essentially, powerless against that, we felt that every cadet who succeeded represented a victory for all cadets.

The reason we had come to Tuskegee was to learn to fly the army way. If a cadet was eliminated because he could not fly the plane, no other cadet could help him. If he was having trouble in his classroom studies, however, his classmates helped him whenever he asked. Similarly, there were no problems between cadets and commissioned officers in training classes. In classrooms, all were students on equal footing. A cadet was never insubordinate to an officer, whether that officer was a classmate or an instructor. The commissioned officer had the power of God, as far as a cadet was concerned.

In my winter uniform, 1943.

In basic flight training, we had the opportunity to fly higher-powered army airplanes. I began basic on September 2, 1943, flying the BT-13A Valiant, a monoplane, meaning it had a single main wing, like most airplanes we see today. It was powered by a 450 horsepower Pratt & Whitney engine. This military aircraft had twice the power of the Stearman biplane I had flown in primary training, but to me it felt like a flying boxcar. It was a less forgiving aircraft.

Sometimes weather restricts a pilot's ability to see where he is going, so before we were allowed to fly solo, we had to learn to fly by instrument: blind flying. Flying an actual airplane with an instructor, we went under the hood, a device worn on the head that keeps a person from seeing outside the cockpit. While under the hood, as when in clouds, a pilot can't tell where he is or how the plane is oriented from anything other than his instruments. Those dials tell him how he's doing: how fast he's going, whether the wings are level, up, or down. He learns to fly by those instruments.

After we learned to fly the airplane in climbs, dives, and various other maneuvers, we went to the link trainer. The link trainer is a simulated cockpit located inside a building where a pilot can practice maneuvers without the danger of getting hurt. It has all the instruments and indicators of a real airplane, but it cannot be crashed. It can go into a spin, yes, but mistakes there don't kill you. There is radio communication, and the instructor sits alongside. He tells the student what to do: change airspeed, climb, dive, turn to a different heading. There is no view of clouds, horizon—anything. The link really trains a person to fly blind. The instruments tell him which way is up, how to turn, and how to keep the plane level. It's really not that hard, but some men could not do it, so they got eliminated. We had to have the instrument rating.

Basic training also gave us aerobatics instruction. We practiced stalls, spins, and loops. We learned how to perform slow, barrel, and snap rolls. There were other maneuvers we worked on as well. Now we could defy gravity and carve up space in three dimensions, but we always had to respect the limits of our aircraft. We had to know what we were doing.

On November 1, 1943, the last day of basic training, I was up for a sixty-hour instrument check with Captain Coleman. We went up, and I performed maneuvers. I found the beacon, which is the light that guides navigation. While we were in the clouds, flying blind, I was instructed to remove the hood. I just kept flying.

We were coming back into the landing pattern at Tuskegee Airfield when, at one thousand feet, Captain Coleman pulled on the stick and said, "I got it." He pulled a snap roll right in the pattern. He said, "I just became a father this morning, and you passed your instrument check."

If a student had performed a stunt like that in the approach pattern, he would still be in the stockade today!

In basic and advanced training, the instructors were just about as rigid as in primary training. Later, we would have to know how to slide in above, beside, or behind another airplane, and if we did it recklessly, people could get killed. Our instructors tried to train us as well as possible to meet the proficiency requirements. Even more than teaching us to meet requirements, though, they demanded above-average performance from each student. I believe I was well trained.

Later, while flying a high-powered fighter plane, we would not have anyone riding with us, so, when we had satisfied both our instructor and ourselves that we could fly the plane without help, we were allowed to take it around without him. Flying solo is another phase.

I wanted to succeed, to get those golden bars on my shoulder, to get the silver wings. I don't know whether I was the greatest instrument pilot in the world, but I tried to be. At least I learned what I needed to know in order to stay alive in a spin. This saved my life once when I was flying a mission in clouds over Europe. During that mission, we had been told to take "sack time" and head back to the home field because of the weather. With a solid cloud formation up to thirty-five thousand feet, even if the bombers had been able to get through, we would not have been able to recognize them and fly up to meet them without extreme loss of life. The bombers were given permission to go home, and so were we. We started our turn, and I was up on a wing, expecting my leader to turn and dive to a lower altitude to reach clear air. I got turned over too far, though, and my engine cut out; it was not made for inverted flight. The plane dropped into a spin. The number four man called in on the radio, "Counter Blue leader, you just lost your number-two man." Maybe he had seen other pilots lost in the clouds; at any rate, as far as he was concerned, I was gone. There was nothing he could do for me. I was certainly lost from the formation; they didn't know whether I was going to be able to recover or not. It was all up to me and my training. Fortunately, I did recover; I did make it home.

Advanced flight training, the top phase, began for me on November 2, 1943. It included oxygen instruction. Our instructor asked for volunteers for various exercises.

When he needed someone to leave his mask off while everybody else wore one and the oxygen pressure in the advanced trainer was lowered to simulate altitude, I said, "Okay, I'll take my mask off at thirty thousand feet."

As a pilot, when you get to thirty thousand feet and take off your mask, you don't notice anything different. But the oxygen is not there to breathe because the pressure is so low. You just pass out from lack of oxygen. I took off my mask, and the instructor gave me a clipboard and paper and pencil to write my name, rank, and serial number. I was writing, and I was doing fine. Unbeknownst to me, the instructor took away the clipboard at some point. I still had the pencil, and I was still writing. The instructor took away the pencil; I was *still* writing. Then I collapsed.

I volunteered for this training because I wanted to know what might happen if my oxygen went bad at thirty thousand feet while on a mission, and this demonstrated to me and the rest of the class that a pilot will not know when his oxygen has gone bad. There is nothing he can do about it, and there's very little anybody else can do. It happened to me on a combat mission. I was out there as if I were having a good time flying our pattern, bouncing up and down and in and out.

A call on the radio said, "Martin, fix your oxygen mask. Fix your oxygen mask!"

I tugged up the straps a little, but I didn't notice any difference. I was still bobbing and weaving out there.

They said again, "Tighten up your oxygen mask. Turn on full oxygen!"

In this condition, your body simply has no way to tell your brain that you are not getting enough oxygen. But because I obeyed my teammates, everything returned to normal. I was very lucky that I didn't pass out.

I never ground-looped a plane until I got into advanced training. Here we flew the AT-6 Texan, the advanced trainer. On this day, we were at Shorter Auxiliary Field at Shorter, Alabama, about twenty-five miles east of Montgomery. Shorter Field had a 3,560-foot-by-3,270-foot turf landing area, unlike the four 5,000-foot asphalt runways we had at the Tuskegee Army Airfield. We were shooting landing stages, but we were practicing forced landings on a small field under conditions of simulated engine failure. In this process, the pilot approaches the field in a stalled attitude with full power and full flaps, with just enough speed and altitude to clear a string hurdle or some other obstacle, such as a line of trees. The pilot chops the throttle and the plane drops in steep and hard. The idea is to get the least amount of forward speed possible in order to produce the shortest landing roll.

It was November 23, close to graduation—the very worst time to have an accident.

On this landing, the plane started veering, and I thought, "Is this a ground loop? I'm just going to let it go and see what happens."

The plane made a nice little turn before coming to a stop.

My instructor, Lieutenant Phillips, got into the plane and said, "Martin, I'm going to give you the ride of your life."

We took off and came back to Shorter Field. He flew the plane in a circle around the field, inside the boundaries, with the wings vertical. I swear the left wingtip was no more than ten feet off the ground. He flew the circle twice.

He said, "If you don't get by your check, you'll have flown something once!"

I did pass my check—lucky again.

My upper advanced training, the last four and a half weeks before graduation, began on December 6. On December 16, I got to fire the nose cannon at the lime pits for the first time. During the next week, I continued to work hard to hit the target. Finally, on December 23, I got to fire the wing guns. Forget cloud nine; I was on cloud infinity! Now I really was a flying gun. That same day, we returned to Tuskegee Army Airfield from the gunnery range, and that part of my training was over.

When approaching a target, sometimes you do not want to give yourself away. So instead of coming in at five thousand or ten thousand feet, you fly in at fifteen hundred feet at the most, or even lower, just on the treetops, so you can surprise the enemy. We were just about ready to graduate when the instructors decided we should go on a low-altitude cross-country flight. The idea was to take off at timed intervals so that we would not immediately follow the man ahead of us, but some of us ended up following one another. When we came in, some of the guys were too close together. Another instructor did not know we were following orders to do a low-altitude flight, and he charged the guys who ended up too close together with buzzing. Buzzing was against the rules.

These cadets were court-martialed. It didn't matter that they had been told to fly at a low altitude. Our word was no good against that of a white officer, especially in Alabama. A cadet's argument didn't mean any more than any protests of innocence against the claims of an arresting officer. Those men had to stay at Tuskegee for the court-martial while the rest of us were released to go to Selfridge Field, Michigan, after graduation.

Class 44-A was the third class in which training in multiengine planes (i.e., bomber training), was available. That was fine for the bigger pilots who could not sit comfortably when we trained in a P-39. Everyone knew this new bomber unit would not be going into combat anytime soon, though. In fact, it never saw combat. As for me, I wanted a fighter. I wanted to be an ace. As we approached graduation, I got my instructor to enroll me in fighter pilot training rather than bomber training. I knew that girls went for anybody with their wings and bars, but fighter pilots were a bit cockier than the bomber pilots. I really wanted the fighters.

I graduated from the program at Tuskegee in January, 1944. My class started with fifty-two cadets because we had picked up some from a previous class. About six of the fifty-two got washed back to a later class because of things that could be remedied, such as medical problems, maybe a broken arm. It meant that they would graduate about a month later. But twenty-one classmates were washed out—completely eliminated from the program. Only twenty-five graduated out of the original fifty-two, and only eight of us went overseas as replacement pilots. The fact that so few Black pilots were allowed to graduate and go overseas meant that we would have to fly more missions without rest, since there were fewer replacement pilots to step in. We also flew more total missions than our white counterparts.

Class 44-A
I am on the left, front row.

I was honorably discharged from the service as a cadet on January 6, 1944. Technically, if I had known, I could have left the service honorably at that point and gone home! But I stayed to receive my wings and commission at the graduation ceremony, and I reentered the service as a second lieutenant army officer (AO) in the army air corps on January 7, 1944.

Graduation photo, prop and wings insignia on my shirt collar.

My father and sister Lillian came down to Tuskegee, some miraculous way, to see me graduate. I had located rooms for them and introduced them to the one civilian I knew. I saw them at the ceremony, however briefly, and gave my sister the government's set of pilot's wings to pin on me. There was a superstition that bad things might happen if your girlfriend pinned on your wings, but I didn't have to worry about that anyway. I let my sister do it. Then my folks disappeared. It may have crossed my mind that this could be the last time I would ever see them, but I did not really believe that. With the bravado unique to the young and inexperienced, I knew nothing bad could happen to me overseas.

Now a commissioned officer, I was a pilot, an aspiring hero, and cannon fodder—a cog in the US war machine. I wasn't certain how I felt about going to war, but one thing was certain: I would need more moxie to be ready for combat, and that started with more training.

CHAPTER 4

COMBAT TRAINING

After graduation, we were placed into what was called fighter transition, where we had to log ten hours in a fighter aircraft before we left Tuskegee. This was when I flew the Curtiss P-40 Warhawk, with its famous "shark mouth," for the first time. Some German aircraft during both world wars had been painted with faces, but the image we know now first appeared on British P-40 Tomahawks in North Africa and was then picked up by the Flying Tigers in Burma and China.[19] Even our well-worn castoffs, probably sent from other US bases receiving new aircraft, were painted with shark teeth.

"You got your wings and bars," we were told, "now fly the damn P-40!" As brand-new pilots, we studied the operations manuals and pictures of the plane. We took blindfold tests to acquaint ourselves with all the switches, controls, and levers we might need to fly without taking our eyes off the action outside the cockpit. This included the manual crank to let the wheels down for an emergency landing. The day to try out this baby came on January 12, 1944. I was the second in my class to get a turn at it.

Flying a new type of plane by myself without an instructor on board, every nerve on edge, was one of the greatest thrills in my life. The P-40 flew beautifully using high power settings, the top numbers on the dials where I'd never seen the needles sitting still before—fifty-plus inches of manifold pressure, 2,600 rpm inching up in green on the dials, making the pedals

---

[19] Cory Graff, "How the Curtiss P-40 Got That Wicked Shark Grin," *Smithsonian Air & Space Magazine*, April 2020, https://www.smithsonianmag.com/air-space-magazine/when-shark-bites-180974484/.

and stick a bit stiffer. All that power made the plane move even with my feet on the brakes.

Of course we had been taught landing settings as well as takeoff power settings, control settings for flaps, engine cowl procedure, and other important things, and we had committed them to memory. After a high-speed survey of the instrument panel, pushing back on the stiffening rudder pedals, vibration like I'd never felt before, all that power screaming, moving down the runway, suddenly I did not feel the aircraft rolling anymore. I smoothed into the air at a liftoff speed too fast to read the number dials. *Okay, check it at next glance.* Then came that mule kick of the cowl flaps lever on my left arm—I'd never felt that before! And now I was really flying. I said to myself, "I'm home, baby!"

As I climbed up above the nearby training areas, trimming the ship, throttling back, and retracting the wheels, with towns and roads stretching away, I was in *my* P-40. I was pilot, second lieutenant, testing a 250-mph dive; tomorrow it would be 400 mph. *Bring on your Luftwaffe; I am here to win this war. I can fly this plane anywhere and shoot any enemy out of the sky. We'll test it today and wring it out tomorrow with steep turns and climbs.*

I got going, and before I knew it, I was over Notasulga, twenty miles away; I got my bearings and flew the airplane. It was a beautiful ship in the air, very easy to handle once I got up there and got everything trimmed away. I didn't perform any aerobatics, but I did everything short of that. Honestly, the plane still scared me just a little. The aircraft I'd flown before had radial engines that extended only a little way in front of me. Now, here was this great big inline engine, so long it looked as if it went on forever.

I really had a ball. *Jeepers, there's nothin' to this airplane. I was master! I was the greatest pilot in the world!* At the end of the flight, we—my P-40 and I—flew across the field high. We let down to enter the pattern at some legal level, made a steep turn showing off all our silhouette, and contacted the tower. The area had been cleared for the first-time P-40 pilots. All the field operations people were somehow on the alert. *If you wanna stay alive, be on the alert for landing instructions and prepare for Caesar's triumphal march into Rome.*

But life isn't always the way you imagine it. Landing my chariot that time was not accomplished with the smooth, devil-may-care *skee-eet* of the rubber kissing the pavement that I had expected. Putting down six thousand pounds at around 90 mph was interesting—an undelightful experience in which things could have gone terribly wrong.

I came in to land, and I stalled this baby out at five feet off the ground. That's when trouble started. Five feet is far enough for a wing to drop, and the left wing dropped. The plane landed on the left wheel and bounced over to the other wheel. The fight was on. I came in to land heading northeast. I dragged that left wing through the grass on the side of the runway. I fought with the rudder, the stick, the throttle, the brakes. Finally, I got this thing straightened out—heading northwest. That was ninety degrees from my initial heading and on the other runway.

I was still fighting this airplane. Finally, I said to myself, "Okay, I'll take over now."

I cut the throttle, pulled back on the stick, and stood on the brakes. It stopped. Finally. The tail came up. The propeller did not hit the ground. The plane was in flying position, standing on two wheels. Finally, the tail dropped and the rear wheel hit the ground. I taxied back to the hangar.

The instructor met me and said, "Why don't you let me call your mother and tell her you're not going to fly anymore?"

I said, "No, I'm going to fly this thing."

Another guy, Sanford Perkins, a class leader who had soloed more successfully, said, "I'm not going to fly this thing any more today. I'm going home to make love to my wife this afternoon. I'll see you guys tomorrow."

I went up and flew the airplane again that afternoon, and on my second landing, I really greased it in. I stalled it out about six inches off the ground and landed it in perfect three-point position, the way it would sit on the ground. That was the last of my trouble with the P-40. I flew all the rest of the required flight activities, including a dive at four hundred miles per hour, then straight up, up, up, and into a slow roll at twelve thousand feet—any lower might have been suicide—and it was all a piece of cake.

I liked flying the P-40 at that time. After I came back from overseas as an instructor at Tuskegee, however, I had a little incident that changed my mind. The war was over by then, but there were no P-51s at the field, just a couple of P-40s. Generally, the white instructors would take the P-40s for weekend trips. They would come back Sunday night and be ready for classes Monday. Black instructors would get the planes to fly during the week.

I climbed into the P-40 and took it up alongside one of the east–west air lanes over central Alabama. A four-engine commercial plane was flying along, and here I was, a hot fighter pilot back from the war in my P-40.

Ah, I will have me some fun, I thought. *I'll get alongside of him, wiggle my wings so he won't think I'm attacking him, and gradually slide in close to him. Nothing in a threatening manner, just letting him know I'm there.*

So I did this, sitting out there, looking at the people with their noses stuck to the windows. Then the pilot poured the coal to his four-engine plane and I poured coal to my old P-40—and he walked away from me. He had four engines. When he throttled up, he had more power. I went back and landed that P-40 and said good-bye. I never tried to fly it again.

At the time of my graduation, however, we thought the P-40 was a great airplane. This was the plane the 99th Fighter Squadron was using so effectively overseas. We flew the P-40 until our assignment to Selfridge Army Air Base in Michigan on February 5, 1944. I was ready to go, eager to continue my training and more than ready to leave the prejudice of the Deep South behind. This time I would not even have to deal with the segregation of the railroad system, because three of us had arranged to ride with another officer who had a car. All we had to do was take turns with the driving.

The guy with the car had been driving to Chicago about every other week, and his access to all that gasoline was the source of a lot of speculation among the rest of us. We thought he was a spy. The cadet corps really did seem infiltrated. We saw light-skinned cadets who had no apparent roots in Black communities disappear like washouts, and we believed they went on to undercover assignments elsewhere. In fact, a fellow in my preflight class later told me that when he got to primary flight training, he was told that he would not be allowed to graduate from primary—that he would be a spy instead. They gave him a special set of identification wings to pin on his shirt collar, and he was told to let them know about any troublemakers in the class or anybody who was working for any other nation or group. He went on to become a police officer in Chicago.

Whether the guy with the car was a spy or not I can't say for sure. I drove with him as far as Nashville. There I planned to visit my college roommate, who was now a chemistry professor at Tennessee State College for Blacks. Louis introduced me to several associates, and then he introduced me to one young doll who I thought might make a future companion. I was not ready for marriage at that time, of course. Why should I get married only to go off to war and get killed, leaving my wife with a kid and $10,000 to be grabbed for by a bunch of other guys? I would just name my plane for her and look her up in the future. But life has a way of moving on. I ended up naming the plane after someone else, and I never saw this girl again.

A day later, I caught a train to Chicago, then another one to Dubuque. I found that my old buddies had gone off to war, and I knew they were not coming home to see me, so I visited my high school to show off my wings and commission. I said hello to a few teachers, received congratulations, and was awarded a high school team sweatshirt. People greeted me with polite smiles, but some, I knew, were not especially happy to see me. Dubuque had many German families who had connections in cities where bombs were being dropped daily.

After a day or so in Dubuque, I headed to Detroit and Selfridge Field. I was happy to be in the North again and thrilled at the prospect of getting a new airplane. I arrived there on my twenty-fifth birthday, February 9, 1944, as part of the newly formed 553rd Fighter Squadron. This squadron was activated to provide replacements for pilots already deployed in the 99th Pursuit Squadron and the 332nd Fighter Group.

Me, on left, with Frank Roberts and Alex Jefferson.
Selfridge Field, March 1944.

"Big D" was a welcome surprise. Barracks at Selfridge Field were segregated, and Lufbery Hall, the officers' club, was off limits to Black officers. But Detroit, at least, offered civilization. It had paved streets, sidewalks, brick buildings, and a great downtown, with late-night streetcars and buses. This was where I got together with classmates when we had the time. O'Neil and Alex Jefferson showed us the "Valley," where we found Black nightclubs and friendly, proud people to welcome us. I was with a bunch of fellas at a tavern when I met Helen Cole; she was there with a bunch of girls. Soldiers meeting girls at a tavern, having a few drinks and conversation, a few dances—that was it. That was the latest attempt at a conquest. But in Europe, when men were naming their planes after their girlfriends or their wives and I did not have anyone as close as that, Helen Cole came back to mind. Nat King Cole was one of my musical idols, so Helen became, for me, Queen Cole, and that was the name I gave my plane.

Actually, our planes had dual identities. My side said *Queen Cole*, but that plane belonged to her mechanic just as much as she did to me. The other side bore the name *Sweet Eleanor*. Come to think of it, I don't even know what happened to that plane. I was not flying it the day I got shot down, and when I came back, the squadrons were moving to a new location and there was no time to find out anything. I like to think that she got a new name and continued on great adventures. But I was not thinking of any of that when I met Helen in Detroit.

At Selfridge Field, we were introduced to the P-39, the Airacobra. Learning how to fly it was, once again, up to us. We found it to be a great little airplane, a fun ship that was easy to fly. It had four .30-caliber machine guns and a 37 mm cannon that fired through the prop. It had a tricycle landing gear, which meant wonderful ground visibility in spite of its enormous nose cannon. A pilot did not have to snake back and forth while taxiing; he could see where he was going on the ground. The P-39 was not as fast or as maneuverable as the P-40, but it could fly.

Some liked this plane's maneuverability, its armaments, its structural strength. But the P-39 had some handling problems, so we could not execute loops with it. It could spin out of control. Its top speed was a slow 350 mph, and the turbocharger was not efficient enough to perform well at high altitudes. The P-39 turned out to be useless against the German Messerschmitt 109 or their Focke-Wulf 190. The only place it ever really worked well was in Russian operations against tanks. It was also used a little bit in the South Pacific. But ultimately, for us, it was a toy to get killed in. Cornelius May, the first upperclassman to treat me as an equal at Tuskegee, was killed in a P-39 at Selfridge Field.

Here in the North, we learned to fly in rain and snow squalls and to negotiate icy runways. We also learned combat flying in the P-39, shooting live rounds, including live cannon projectiles. We fired at targets being towed in the air. We fired at ground targets. We did both tight and loose formation flying. We also did rat racing.

Rat racing is simulated combat with an opposing plane. We practiced following another airplane and maneuvering into a position to shoot it down. Four planes would take off, and then the leader would peel off. The second plane would try to get into a position to shoot down the leader. The third plane would maneuver to shoot at the second one, and the fourth man would fire at the third. One of the objectives was to cut off the target from any kind of return. In combat, we would need to use our 37 mm cannon to disable the opposing aircraft, so we practiced firing the nose cannon a lot.

I mentioned Lufbery Hall, the officers' club at Selfridge Field. You see, once a cadet receives his commission, he automatically becomes a paying member of the officers' club. At that time, however, Black officers were not allowed entrance to any club that the white officers used. They were told to wait until a separate facility could be constructed for them. Who could be happy with that answer? Just before my arrival at Selfridge Field, some Black officers tried to use the only officers' club on base at the time. This was right around New Year's Day, 1944.

Lieutenant Milton Henry, along with two other officers, went to the club as part of a coordinated effort to break down the barrier. An attendant seated them and was about to take their order when Col. William Boyd, the base commander, arrived. He used very insulting language to order them out of the club.[20] Lieutenant Henry ended up traveling all the way to Washington to file a complaint of racial discrimination, but he was eventually court-martialed anyway.

In April of 1944, after Lieutenant Henry's trial and before he was found guilty of all charges and discharged, General Frank O. Hunter

---

[20]   Lawrence P. Scott and William M. Womack Sr., *Double V: The Civil Rights Struggle of the Tuskegee Airmen* (East Lansing: Michigan State University Press, 1998), 200.

visited Selfridge Field. General Hunter, born in Savannah, Georgia, was commander of the First Air Force and a decorated World War I flying ace. He called all the Black officers stationed at Selfridge Field into the base theater and said, essentially, that we Blacks were not equal to the whites and could never be that equal, and that there would be no intermingling of the races on the base.

"'This country is not ready or willing to accept a Colored officer as the equal of a White one,' Hunter is quoted as saying. 'You are not in the army to advance your race. Your prime purpose should be in taking your training and fighting for your country. As for racial agitators, they will be weeded out and dealt with.'"[21]

There was no chance to challenge anything after that. The officers' club had already been closed.

We were all grounded for about a week, and the next thing we knew, we had new instructions: "Get packed; you're going to be relocated."

We were put on a train without being told where we were going or when we were going to get there. We were grounded while white pilots from somewhere—any-damned-where—were chosen to ferry the planes from Selfridge Field. About four days later, the train stopped out in the wilderness at Walterboro, South Carolina, about seventy-five miles north-northeast of Savannah.

As you can imagine, tempers were already quite touchy because of the way we had been treated by the war command. At Walterboro, the insults continued and worsened. We were isolated without access even to newspapers or radio. When some tried to desegregate the base theater using the "checkerboard" tactic that had been used successfully at Selfridge Field, they were simply ordered out of the theater.

Training utilized harsh and arbitrary rules. Townspeople refused to allow us to purchase the food and retail merchandise that white personnel could get. In fact, sometimes we had a hard time getting basic services. Of course we pronounced our new location "Walter-damn-boro." It was located in "Defecation" South Caro-damned-lina, Confederate States of America, too. During a war, or in times of intense emotional stress, the military abandons proper English and uses explicit, meaningful terms.

---

21   Scott and Womack, *Double V*, 209.

The southern white power structure, both within the military and in the local community, wanted to keep things the way they had been; they wanted to keep us "in our place." But we had all, by this time, proven ourselves as pilots, as officers, and as men; the instructors who led us, members of the famed 99th Pursuit Squadron, had been tested and tempered in the fires of war. We had found our power. To try to subjugate us once more was no more possible than forcing a genie back into a bottle. Of course there was friction on the ground. We had no recreational outlets, no way to defuse the tension created by the discrimination we found there.

But we were flying again. We started flying formation and aerial gunnery. Our instructors had been used primarily in dive-bombing and strafing assignments overseas, so we learned dive-bombing and strafing. We thought we were pretty good at it too. By the time our unit arrived in Europe, we were assigned a totally different type of work, but such was the fluid nature of war.

On our first day's flying after the failed attempt to desegregate the base theater, we buzzed the mayor's home and the water tower next door at nine o'clock on a Sunday morning. I don't know whether our leaders knew we were buzzing the mayor's house. As far as I knew, we were simply recovering from a dive-bombing pass at the training base. But the first day we flew at Walterboro, we went out to the range, went down and dived, and then we pulled out in front of the town right at treetop level about nine o'clock in the morning. After that, we went back to the dive-bombing range and repeated it. Evidently we buzzed the control tower at the base as well.[22]

Officials wanted to nail the flight leader for buzzing the control tower, but they mixed up the records and thought it was Captain Clark who had led that flight. They wanted to court-martial him. I was in the flight; it was led by Captain Charles Dryden, our instructor, who was one of the original twenty-five members of the 99th Pursuit Squadron, as was Captain Clark.

---

[22] Others have called it a "simulated low-altitude, high-speed attack" focused on the water tower—which just happened to be next to the mayor's house. The "attack" shook every house in the neighborhood. Scott and Womack, *Double V*, 217.

Anderson, Gordon, Clark, Doswell, Ellis, Dryden.

Captain Dryden had proved his mettle in war. He had participated in the battle for Pantelleria.[23] He spoke up and said, "Don't railroad Clark. I did it; I led that flight, and I'll face the court-martial." He was a great flight leader, besides having flown combat overseas. With him, we had tasted "war" in our training, flown planes in show formation, shot .30-caliber guns and 37 mm cannons out over the Atlantic. We were sure he could beat the charges, but that just shows how little we knew.

Dryden was convicted of violating the Ninety-Sixth Article of War—buzzing the base—and sentenced to dismissal from the service. When a review showed he had not been allowed all his rights, however, a second trial was held, and he was convicted again but not dismissed from the service. Instead, he was fined three months' pay, confined to base for three months, and denied promotion for one year. While still not delivering what could be called a light sentence, the retrial saved Dryden's career. He ended up staying in the army air force, serving in the Korean War, and retiring as a colonel in 1962.[24]

The buzzing incident was not the only way in which we crossed the white power structure at Walterboro. There were no live .30-caliber rounds on base for our airplanes, so one day after a training flight, our white flight leader took us to another base. After we had secured the ammunition we

23 Chris Bucholtz, *332nd Fighter Group—Tuskegee Airmen* (Long Island City, NY: Osprey Publishing, 2007), 21.
24 Bucholtz, *332nd Fighter Group,* 124.

needed, our leader took us to lunch at the white officers' club. In dining there, of course, we broke the code. I was in that group, and such a thing never happened again at Walterboro. The other flights were taken far afield by truck to a Black infantry camp.

Our instructors told us that while on the ground overseas, treatment within the unit was tolerable. These were combat veteran officers now ranking as first lieutenants or captains with full tours of duty behind them. They had faced the enemy and survived any number of misfortunes in war, yet now they had come back to find themselves under the authority of white shavetail officers who had not seen any action. Some of our instructors volunteered for another tour of duty rather than subject themselves to this indignity.

In a letter to a college classmate back in Iowa I said, in part,

> Two weeks ago, our whole organization was transferred to this hole down in South Car-o-damn-lina where nobody likes it at all, and life under the heat and prejudice is most depressing and at times revolting. Conditions are such that I often stop to wonder what I'm in the army fighting for and why I must go overseas to fight instead of fighting here. Anyway, I finished my training here and I'm sure conditions affecting one's mind can't be any worse in combat.
>
> I know all of this isn't the news you want, but I just wanted you to know what I'm up against, not as a college graduate but as a Negro. My world and yours, though they should be getting closer, are drifting further apart every minute. It will be up to fellows like you to start them back together.[25]

An incident in Walterboro that nearly turned tragic occurred when one of our instructors, Captain Spann Watson, had an altercation at a local car repair shop when he tried to get a tire repaired. The Black mechanic he had spoken with had offered several appointments, and having chosen one, he returned later that day to pick up his tire, only to find it not ready. When

---

[25] Letter to college classmate Verne Hudek, May 18, 1944 (*African American Heritage Foundation of Iowa*, Cedar Rapids).

he asked why not, a white man interrupted to tell the mechanic to continue working on his car. He slapped Captain Watson when he objected.

Watson had already had to deal with white men trying to pick up his wife, and this combat veteran was in no mood for insult now. He dropped the tire he was holding and knocked the man down with a hard right to the jaw. Unfortunately, this man happened to be the mayor. Watson immediately found himself surrounded by angry white mechanics and customers. He was able to fend them off temporarily, but when he noticed one man leaving to get what Watson knew would be a gun, he left the fight and ran to the nearest military police station.

Watson told the two white MPs on duty to get their guns ready and call the base for backup. A few minutes later, the mayor of Walterboro arrived with a mob and demanded that Watson be turned over to them. No matter that he was under the army's jurisdiction, they were intent on a lynching.

Fortunately, the base commander, Colonel Prince, arrived in time with backup. After getting each side of the story, the commander promised the mayor and his police officers that the army would take their official complaints and prosecute Captain Watson. He told Watson privately that he believed him, and Watson was ordered to leave Walterboro that evening under cover of darkness. Watson picked up his wife and headed north to join the 477th Bombardment Group in Kentucky.[26]

As any civilian knows, an army camp has lots of weapons, but there are no rounds lying around because regulations cover their ease of access. Now, because there was concern that the mayor's mob might try to come onto the base in search of Captain Watson, the men in charge of weapons secretly passed out ammunition to the officers. That way, if things did get heated, we would be able to defend ourselves.

Fortunately, civilians never came onto the base, and life returned to what passed as normal. But our circumstances at Walterboro certainly were enough to get us riled up. They were setting us up for war!

We had arrived at Walterboro in early May, and now the month was nearly gone. We'd had no news from outside the base, no social life, and now, in preparation for departure, we were restricted to the base. We had had to turn in our ID cards, the ones with our picture and thumbprint

---

26   Scott and Womack, *Double V*, 219–20.

under plastic that we were never supposed to be without. We were not yet in Europe, but our turn was coming. It was here; it was booked.

We had no officers' club, but in the barracks we could play cards for sixteen hours straight. Soft drinks were in great supply in the Coke machines, and half pints of Midnight Express (the worst alcohol I have ever tasted) stood around, only one-fourth sampled. But we had nothing to inspire us until a few non-flying officers organized a trip to town.

We borrowed ID cards from owners who bore some physical similarity to us to show at the gate, and then we were off. Why shouldn't we have a little fun before we went off to war? About five of us piled into a car and rode maybe thirty miles out, away from Walterboro. We enjoyed the sights of the city, found a nightclub, had a few drinks, and returned to base. So to bed and no troubles.

CHAPTER 5

TRIP TO WAR

Out of fifty-two cadets in our original class at Tuskegee, only eight of us would be sent overseas as replacement pilots in the 332nd Fighter Group: Driver, Duke, Jackson, Jefferson, Martin, O'Neil, Perkins, and Roberts. We also picked up three who were washed back from an earlier class and three who were moved up from the class behind us, so we had a fourteen-man shipment to go overseas.

We left Walterboro by train on May 29. On the way, a journal bearing overheated and started a fire by one of the wheels—a condition known as a "hotbox." The fire was extinguished and the problem fixed soon enough, but the diversion gave us a little time to get out and look around at the southern landscape we were so glad to leave behind. Then we continued on our journey to Camp Patrick Henry in Warwick County, Virginia, our port of embarkation for overseas assignment.

There were a lot of people at Camp Patrick Henry, a whole lot of troops, and a great big PX, and we saw guys walking around in paratrooper boots. These were some beautiful boots, and we thought we might need something like that in case we had to jump out of a plane. But then we heard that the paratroopers did not like that. Paratroopers were white, and they had attacked some Black soldiers who had the nerve to buy standard army-issue paratrooper boots, so we elected not to buy them after all.

Before shipping out, we needed instructions and equipment. They gave us our guns, .45 caliber pistols with holsters. They also gave us bayonets— and no, the bayonets were not meant to be attached to the .45s! They gave us each a canteen, a backpack, a helmet, a helmet liner, and a mess kit. At

Tuskegee, we did not know what a mess kit was all about. We had never had to eat out of or wash one. Now we were told how to open and close our mess kits.

We also learned a few other things, such as how to make a backpack with a blanket roll, and we saw a movie about boarding a ship. If you have to board a ship on a rope ladder, you do not want to put your hands on the horizontal ropes. Use the vertical ropes; otherwise, somebody might step on your hand and you could end up in the water with your backpack and everything. They also said that before going up or down the rope ladder, we should remove our helmets. Otherwise, if we fell into the water, our helmets could get caught in the current, jerk our heads, and even break our necks. That was a word to the wise.

While at Camp Patrick Henry, we had freedom to move around, so we decided to visit Hampton Institute, which was nearby. There I ran into a fellow, Herbert DaCosta, whom I had left two years before in college. He was now an instructor at Hampton. He had very bad eyes and was not going into the service anywhere. He introduced us to some of his friends and took us out to somebody's house on the bay, where they held a crab feast. These were hard-shelled crabs; our hosts boiled them in a washtub, then showed us how to break them open to get out the "dead man." We had a great time eating crab and drinking beer.

Since we were allowed to go into town at night, of course we went nightclubbing. And, of course, we found that a lot of the girls were amenable. At Hampton Institute, in a nice part of the campus, there was a tree with a low horizontal limb, and that limb, we were told, was the ruination of the college education of many young couples. A dean patrolled this tree, and every time she caught a couple there exercising their rights, she said, "Go ahead and finish, because you won't be here tomorrow."

Anyway, we went to town at night and found girls in nightclubs. Every night when we left, we would say, "We'll be back tomorrow; be ready about seven thirty or eight."

One night when we told them that, they said, "No, you won't be in town tomorrow night."

How come?

"Well, we saw a ship pull into the channel; you'll be gone tomorrow."

And they were right. We embarked for Europe aboard the USS *General W. A. Mann* on June 4, 1944.

On the ship, we bunked in a small cabin below the main deck. We did not have to climb up a rope ladder; we walked up a gangplank and went to our cabin. It was small, with bunks for sixteen people stacked four levels high. Since there were only fourteen of us, we had a little extra space to stow our stuff. But there was no porthole.

This was a big ship; I think it had about twelve thousand soldiers on it. About two thousand of them were second lieutenants, and we were all on one level below the main deck. I swore that when I came back I was going to be a captain and have a cabin above the main deck, where at least I'd have a porthole I could open in the daytime to get some air. When I returned, however, there were a thousand first lieutenants, and we were right back down there.

The ship departed, and we were out on the ocean, just out of sight of land. The ship would go up and hold there, and then it would go down. Then it would go up, hold, and then go down. It made us a little queasy. The only place to feel good was up in the bow, where we could watch the ship go up and down; then the drop was at least not unexpected.

Everybody was apprehensive about something. I kept thinking that if the public knew we were going overseas, German spies might know it too. We just knew that a sub would be waiting for us somewhere out there.

The *General W. A. Mann* had been an ocean liner, so it sported a promenade, which we could walk around, above the main deck. There was also an area where we could play deck tennis. It is played with two people on a side and a metal ring that you toss over the net; the other side is supposed to catch it and toss it back.

Frank Roberts, my buddy, and I got pretty good at this. We spent hours there, playing anybody who wanted to play, and we could get pretty sweaty. Unfortunately, the showers were saltwater, so they didn't help much. There was talk about a saltwater soap, but I never saw any.

We also had a big lounge available to us. We could go into the lounge and sing songs to keep up our courage. We could also play bridge. We could play poker over in the corners, or we could sit and smoke and talk, and sit and smoke and talk. If we got tired of that, we could go out to the bow of the ship and watch the water.

Once away from shore, the waves were not so bad. There was not so much movement on the boat, so we could watch the water down below. A little farther south, there were flying fish. I don't know why flying fish fly, but they precede the boat as though the boat is chasing them. I never saw any sharks or any other big fish chasing them. Flying fish were something to watch when we were not looking for an enemy periscope.

And we were looking for periscopes. Word was that this ship could outrun a torpedo or a submarine, but I don't see how it could have outrun a shot from the side. We were supplied dingy blue-gray life vests and were told to keep them with us at all times.

"If you fall or jump overboard, the ship cannot stop," we were told. "We can't risk twelve thousand lives to save one life."

This was just another indication to us that we were dog meat. So we hung on to our life vests and hoped the ship would not be sunk, because if it were, there would be a hell of a fight for a seat in a lifeboat.

We passed the time hoping that we would not encounter any subs. The boat had a couple of gun crews for defense against any attack, and they practiced every day. They would send up a black balloon, and after the balloon reached a certain height, they would open up on it with a five-inch gun. This made a lot of noise, and of course sound travels over water. The explosions made big black puffs of smoke, too, that floated in the air for a little while.

We weren't allowed to throw cigarette butts overboard so the enemy could say, "Look, they went that way!" However, the smoke and explosions might as well have been a trail of bread crumbs left all across the ocean. We couldn't help but wonder whether a submarine might be out there listening and looking for these signs, waiting for us.

It is worth noting that, on the USS *General W. A. Mann*, eating and the use of facilities was not segregated. We got in line in front of or behind anybody. We got our food on a tray and sat down anywhere we liked. Then we dumped our trays and went on about our business. We got only two meals a day; they did not want to overfeed us.

It took us nine days to cross the ocean. We passed through the Strait of Gibraltar and arrived at the Port of Oran, Algeria, on Tuesday, June 13, 1944. Here on the north coast of Africa I stepped onto foreign soil for the first time. We disembarked and went to a little camp where there didn't seem to be many people, either white or Black. From there we were free to go into town or to the beach.

The day I visited the beach, the undertow was too strong for swimming, but I got my feet wet in the Mediterranean anyway. We also went to the theater in town and a couple of other places. It was important not to go alone and to carry a loaded .45. We were told not to go into any side streets or alleys, because we could get killed just for our clothes and shoes.

From Oran, we headed to Naples on a British ship. It carried a thousand troops, and still the fourteen of us were the only Black men on board. This boat had not been converted into a troop carrier like the USS *General W. A. Mann*; it was still in its original state except that it had been painted gray so as not to be so visible. We had staterooms, a lounge, and baths. There was an Indian steward, and if you asked, he would draw you a bath of nice, hot, fresh water. The British also insisted on serving tea every afternoon. They would call us to the lounge for a big tray of cookies and cake with hot tea. We just lay back and enjoyed ourselves for the three or four days it took to make this trip.

The bay of Naples, which we soon came to speak of as Napoli, is surrounded by mountains with views of the sea beyond. Our ship tied up to a huge set of piers that had been fashioned from the side or bottom plates of ruined and unidentifiable vessels from various nations, welded together with beams by the Allied Command. The fighting had ended in Naples not long before we got there, so there had not been time to do anything but use these things as they were. The Germans had taken everything they could, including any bombs that might have been there. We were all ordered to pick up our bags and carry them on this slippery steel walkway to shore.

Our arrival was noticed with whistles and cheers by all kinds of troops. An Indian Gurkha walked by with a large, shiny knife hanging on his belt. We nodded, not knowing what the saluting rules were. The Allies were running the place now. The civilian population, I imagine, must have hated seeing more and more foreign soldiers flooding in.

Once on solid ground, we took our bags and boarded trucks for a ride up the mountain to Bagnoli, a western quarter of Naples, and then to the grounds of what we knew as Bagnoli University. Our convoy drove through huge red stone gates onto the university grounds, where we were assigned cots in a classroom. This area was fenced and guarded, we were told, so that the locals would not be able to come in and rob us during the night.

We arrived in Italy in late June, so the mess was outside. Serving tables were set up. We provided the mess kits, which we had to learn to clean properly. Someone had figured out that we could avoid getting dysentery if we scraped the yellow stuff off the surface with steel wool, then dipped the kits in hot water. Here at Bagnoli, by the way, was where I had the best coffee that I would taste anywhere in the army during all three years and eleven days that I served.

The area, as I said, was fenced, and the garbage cans were near the fence. When we finished eating, we were supposed to drop any leftover food into a garbage can. But on the other side of the fence were fifty or more little Italian kids. Each of them had a bucket or pot, and they begged us to give them our garbage, right on top of somebody else's garbage: the bread we had not eaten, the meat, the potatoes—whatever.

"Just put it in there, Joe," they said. The Allies had not yet set up a food supply for the Italians, and they were starving.

After the first meal, I took extra food to give to the kids and, by extension, their families. Some of my buddies did the same. But some of the other guys would not give them the garbage off their plates. They would even bang their plates extra loud on the garbage can as if to say, "I'm five thousand miles from home and not happy about it, and you ain't even going to get my garbage."

The next day, we discovered what a wreck Naples had become. We walked down the promenade. The marble walkway was edged by a balustrade, which outlined the shore. Both had been badly damaged by bombing. Trucks and manpower had cleared the roadway, and now chunks of marble littered its edges. The people on the street were somewhat dirty and dazed. No one seemed to have a real purpose except for the young hustlers selling women at almost any price one wanted to bargain for.

We were in Naples for a few days, but there was not much to see because of the damage. Nearby, Mount Vesuvius had erupted only three months earlier, destroying nearby towns and smothering the Allied airbase at Pompeii. The eruption killed twenty-six civilians and displaced nearly twelve thousand. It also destroyed eighty-eight B-25 bombers from the US

340th Bombardment Group.[27] From my perspective three months later, however, Naples seemed pretty safe and even boring.

Black officers from the quartermaster department had made friends and acquaintances. They had taken over a few undamaged homes and had created private clubs here and there. The friendships of fraternity brothers from various Black colleges back home had created the right connections, and the brothers were helping others enjoy some relaxation. Of course we were invited to join them, but I soon found that, because I was broke and had no coterie of Black college connections, Napoli had nothing much to offer me.

In contrast to the postwar despair of Naples, the Isle of Capri beckoned. It sat way out in the bay, providing a rest camp at the time for Twelfth Air Force pilots. I so would have liked to see the place whose breathtaking beauty had made it a resort sought out by the rich and famous since the time of the Roman Republic. I had come of age singing the popular song of that name. But a powerboat and a white skin were required to get there, and I had neither. It would have helped to know, as we learned months later, that the 332nd did have a rest camp a few miles farther up the mountain from Naples. It wasn't the Isle of Capri, but it was decent.

The air corps had not forgotten us; the war was waiting. After three or four days in Naples, we were all told to pack our gear for the next leg of our journey. In the late afternoon, the fourteen of us found our boxcar—a clean one, thank goodness, no farm animals having preceded us—and three boxes of K-rations, the first I had seen, were thrown in with us. The contents of the boxes divided quite evenly among us, we spaced our bags and rolled off into the night.

Every fifteen to twenty minutes, the train would stop at yet another little town. As the evening progressed, I decided I wanted some hot food. The next time the train stopped, I took three cans of K-ration up to the engine and made a deal with the engineer. I would give him one if he would heat up two for me. He agreed. At the next stop, I took my two hot cans of K-ration back to the boxcar and started eating. The other guys jumped on

---

27   Sara E. Pratt, "Benchmarks: March 17, 1944: The Most Recent Eruption of Mount Vesuvius," *Earth: The Science Behind the Headlines* (March 15, 2016), https://www.earthmagazine.org/article/benchmarks-march-17-1944-most-recent-eruption-mount-vesuvius.

the idea. They took their K-rations up to the engine and made a deal to get them at the next stop. Well, the train stopped and these guys jumped out of the boxcar and ran to get their hot meals. This time, though, the engine had pulled away before they got there, taking their K-rations with it. Nothing could be done about it, so they had to content themselves with what was left.

We slept all night in our boxcar as the train rolled across Italy. The next morning, we were riding down the Adriatic side of the mountains when we noticed a high-power line strung alongside the tracks. Each of us had about thirty rounds of .45 ammo, so we thought we should have some pistol practice.

Most guys in the service had been scored for marksmanship during their training routines, but for the flying officers, training was a little different. Our commanding officers got our class into formation, marched us onto the pistol range, and said, "Here's a .45; there's the target." He then told us to line up and fire a number of rounds slow-fire and a number of rounds rapid-fire. That was it. We marched back to the barracks, and they said we were qualified as pistol marksmen. But anyone who has fired a .45 knows it takes a little training before you know how to handle it.

Now, on the train, since we had both .45s and ammunition, and since the power line running alongside was equipped with beautiful porcelain insulators, we decided that this was the time to practice our marksmanship. We started firing at the insulators. Everybody on that side of the train stuck their heads out, wondering whether we were getting attacked. We just kept banging away at our targets. One guy finally hit one, and the whole train cheered.

Eventually, we rolled into the Foggia railroad marshaling yard. Our little group sat there for hours until, finally, a six-by-six truck arrived from our airfield. Relieved to be on our way again, we climbed into the back with our T-4 bags, backpacks, and barracks bags. The trip to Ramitelli took us through more mountains, and rounding a particular curve, we came upon a couple of wrecks. A tank and a truck had been abandoned, wrecked, on the side of the road. But where were the rifles stuck in the ground with the helmets on them, the way they honored dead soldiers during World War I? We saw nothing like that.

We did meet a truck along the way that was coming back from the 332nd. I was glad to see a fellow I knew from Cedar Rapids riding on it.

He was now in the 100th Fighter Squadron. My sister and brother-in-law lived in Cedar Rapids, and this guy told me that my brother-in-law was driving a truck in the quartermaster corps near Naples. I took this to mean that he was relatively safe, so I was satisfied. We got our news where and when we could.

Our contingent arrived at Ramitelli, Italy, on June 28, 1944. As we jumped off the truck, we saw P-47 Thunderbolts back from a mission coming in to land.

I had always wanted to fly one of these. I said, "Oh boy, here's my chance to check out a Jug!"

"No," we were told, "you will have to wait for your P-51."

It turned out that six days before our arrival, Major General Nathan Twining, commander of the Fifteenth Air Force, had directed the 332nd Fighter Group to trade their P-47 Thunderbolts for P-51 Mustangs. The first P-51s arrived at Ramitelli two days before we did. The last P-47 mission would be flown two days after. The first mission the 332nd undertook in the P-51s occurred on July 4, just eight days after the new planes were first brought to Ramitelli.

One of the squadron pilots was flying a P-51 when we arrived. He was doing all kinds of aerobatics and slow rolls at low altitude, but then he flew into the ground and got himself killed. They wouldn't let us walk over to see the wreckage. None of the new guys were allowed to see it, and I don't know that many of the seasoned pilots really wanted to.

The next day, Major Edward Gleed welcomed us. He said, and I'm paraphrasing of course, "You saw something yesterday that we don't like. This is a waste of life. This guy had no business getting himself killed." Then he went on to say, "I know you guys are hot pilots and you want to win the war, but don't do what that guy did. We've got a job for you to do. If you want to show us how hot you are, go up in a plane, find a road, and dive down on one side of the road, into the ground. Fly your plane under this road, come up out of the hole, and then fly back here and land and tell us about it. We'll climb into trucks and drive out there and look at what you've done. Until you know you can do that, don't try it. There's no sense in throwing your life away. Welcome to the 332nd."

The men from Class 44-A assigned to the 100th Squadron were Duke, Jackson, Martin, O'Neil, Perkins, and Roberts, plus two men from 43-K,

Gamble and Thompson. We were taking over the cots of men no longer there either because they had been killed or they had finished their tour of duty.

That evening, the eight of us went as a group to the mess hall. Did the pilots we met there make us feel welcome? Did they say, "Glad to see you," or "Thanks for coming to help out"? Not exactly.

What we got was a disgruntled "Where have you been? We've been waiting for you," and "It's your flight now!"

So much for esprit de corps. Every one of us was speechless. These men were bone tired and grumpy, but did that mean that we could not work together? Were we really supposed to fly on their wings to protect and save them after a welcome like that? I don't remember what we ate that evening, but I knew then that we really had arrived at the war.

We had had six months of combat training, and now, overseas, we had a couple of weeks to get used to our location and the new plane, again without any real training in it, before we went on a mission. We were provided some tech orders and maybe a few words of wisdom from somebody who had already flown it: "This is the throttle and some other controls; this is the way you handle it," and so on. We were told the manifold pressure and the rpm settings to use. But basically we were on our own, as before.

I climbed into the P-51 and immediately thought, *I'm in the AT-6!*

The P-51 was like the advanced trainer but with a long nose. All the instruments were in the same place. The controls were pretty much the same. There was a different oxygen system, which did not matter, and a slightly different radio.

But my reaction was "I'm home! This is the airplane I want to fly!"

I flew the thing without ever reading any tech orders.

Years later, a man told me this was impossible. In all his flying days, every time he went out to fly a new airplane, somebody checked his green card to make sure that he had read the tech orders and was very knowledgeable about the plane before he took off. What his "green card" was I do not even know. Would I have been able to stick it onto the instrument panel and have it execute for itself?

The P-51 Mustang was a beautiful airplane. It was, some say, the best fighter plane that the US Air Forces ever produced. It had a Rolls-Royce Merlin engine, which gave it outstanding high-altitude performance. Drop tanks, also known as external tanks or belly tanks, could be added and then discarded when empty. This gave the Mustang a range of over sixteen hundred miles. The D model, which I would use on my last mission, had six wing-mounted .50-caliber machine guns, a maximum speed capability of 440 miles per hour, and an operating ceiling of nearly forty-two thousand feet.

Mind you, even the most beautifully designed airplane has its limits. One afternoon when we were not flying, I was with others, passing the afternoon, when we heard a noise we'd never heard before. A small, flashing, cloudlike something was falling out of the sky, emitting a sound as it fell that grew louder with each second. After a few seconds, the sound stopped. There was a momentary hush, then a loud bang and a flash. This was some sort of explosion. From this silver flash, we saw parts of what looked like a P-51 wing or fuselage, we thought, tumbling earthward. Paper streamers and other debris floated away. No parachute or pilot appeared.

I never heard any official mention of this particular incident, although later there was a name. It was never confirmed that the noise we heard was made by a plane exceeding its "never exceed" speed and destroying itself against the air, although I think that is what we witnessed. This phenomenon is far less likely today with modern engineering, but a pilot does need to pay attention to the limits of his aircraft. Each make and model of plane is redlined with "V_{NE}" on its airspeed indicator for the maximum speed it should be flown, and a pilot never wants to exceed that.

The other fatal accident I witnessed, other than on the day we arrived, occurred when a P-38 and a red-tailed P-51 were having a playful dogfight. The P-38 was not from the 332nd, of course, but neither was it an enemy plane. The two planes kept circling each other. They wound round and round until they ended up at too low an altitude, at which point the P-51 simply pulled out of the fight, leveled off, and flew away. The P-38 was not so lucky. When the pilot tried to pull up, the plane simply stood on its wing and dived straight into the ground.

As if this tragedy were not enough, however, sometime afterward another P-38 flew over our base. One of their regular jobs was to spray for mosquitoes, so this plane's wing tank was probably loaded with highly flammable insecticide when it was "accidentally" dropped from a low altitude. The tank fell on a tent where a 332nd pilot was sleeping, and the resulting fire burned him to death.

After the 99th Fighter Squadron joined the 332nd Fighter Group, our squadron received orders to go to the area where the 99th was based and tell those boys what the P-51 was all about. We had posted just a few flight hours in the P-51 ourselves, but I considered it a great personal honor and one of the thrills of my life to be instructing some of the great pilots of the 99th.

The 332nd Fighter Group got used airplanes at first. The P-51s we were first given were B and C models, which had "greenhouse" canopies that folded back in sections. We got these planes from other squadrons with various identifying paint schemes, so, as required, we painted the tails for our recognition. Our group decided to paint the whole tails of our planes red; that covered all previous markings very well and made us highly recognizable. By the time we got new planes, bomber groups had begun to request the Red Tails for escort.

I don't know if I ever saw the orders sending me to the 100th Fighter Squadron in Italy. I just got in line and followed when my name was called. Honestly, I think the excitement overrode the fear. The day before our first mission, since we were only about two miles from the Adriatic Sea, we decided to go to the beach. But of course you never know how clean the water is, and the next morning I got up and didn't feel right. The doctor said it was sand fly fever and ordered me to bed. So, instead of taking off on that first mission, I went to bed.

Was it first-time jitters? I really don't think so. I got up the next day feeling all right; after that first illness, I was always ready to fly whatever mission they had for me. I was not afraid or sickly, and I did not try to "slide the movement"—flyer slang for not going on missions. I had the idea that nothing was going to hurt me while I was flying. Some of the guys had problems with their oxygen, health, or the cold. I was in fine shape and flying up a storm. I flew twenty-five missions in nothing flat.

Living in a combat zone is interesting, shall we say, for anyone who has never slept in a tent. I did not draw any of my classmates for tent mates. I was assigned to a tent with Reed Thompson from New Rochelle, New York, and Howard Gamble from Charleston, West Virginia, both from the class ahead of mine. One thing not covered in our training was bivouacking, and none of the three of us knew anything about living in a tent. We were never expected to live in the "field" during wartime.

Fortunately, the enlisted men, the EMs, did know about tents. Gamble, Thompson, and I were given a brand-new tent, and the EMs set it up. First, they leveled an area about fifteen feet square. They took some runway matting, something that kept the planes from landing on a dirt or mud field (and one of the main construction items available overseas), and laid that down for our floor. The runway matting had holes in it where the pieces hooked together, so the EMs obtained some belly tank boxes and used the sides of the boxes to cover the runway matting. Now we had a floor that did not have mud or dust on it.

The tent was made for six people. It was very comfortable with just three men in it, each in his chosen space on a side of the tent away from the door. We had each been issued a cot, a footlocker, a sleeping bag, and mosquito netting, the latter of which required some instruction in proper handling so we would not ruin it by poking holes in it. The netting also came with a frame that held it up and around the cot. In addition, we each received a five-gallon water can and a box, formerly a .50-caliber ammunition box, which we used to store our everyday necessities, such as candy and cigarettes. At night, the box also held our gun.

We were about one hundred miles from the front line, so we felt pretty secure. There were people closer to the enemy than we were, so in the case of an attack, somebody running by would have given us pretty good warning if we needed to get up and run. If we were going to form a skirmish line and fight, we would be notified in time to retrieve our guns. Except for flying missions, we lived in a peaceful, if uneasy, situation and in general tried to make the best of things.

Each of us also received a five-gallon oil can with the top cut out. We could set our helmets into it and, voilá! We had washbasins. Yes, besides being a part of our protective gear, our steel helmets were utensils. When we set them on the oil cans, we could put water in them to wash up, shave, or wash clothes. We could find a mirror and hang it on a tent pole to shave inside, or we could take the setup outside into the sunlight to shave, but we did have to shave. Beards would have caused our oxygen masks to leak, and we needed oxygen on every flight.

When the EMs added about two feet of 2×4 lumber to the bottoms of our tent posts and at the corners, suddenly it didn't matter where in the tent we wanted to be; we could stand up straight! This meant that the sides of the tent did not reach the ground, so as soon as the EMs got more belly tank boxes, they added them around the sides. Now we had protection from drafts underneath as well as a tent that was high enough to walk around in. In time, the EMs were able to fashion a door to fit into the flap opening of the tent, which allowed us to enter and exit as though we were living in a house. One day I came back from a mission, and the door was installed and ready to be used, even before cold weather. Of course, even our EMs could not provide indoor plumbing; for toilets, we had the latrines: four-hole outhouses set at various places around the area.

When we got sweaty and wanted to get into clean underwear, we learned to bathe from our helmets. But we were flying four-and-a-half to five-hour missions, and some of the guys who had been flying for six months began to get sore bottoms. So the EMs cut down fifty-five-gallon drums so that when these guys returned from a mission, they could sit and soak their rear ends for some relief.

I didn't need to soak in a bathtub, but I wanted a shower. I got permission from the squadron commander to build one. From some of the guys down on the line, I got an old shell case from a flare, drilled holes in the bottom, and fitted it into a five-gallon oil drum, which I mounted on top of a platform made with the ends of a couple of belly tank boxes. This made two sides of a shower. I had already dug a hole underneath. It should have been four feet deep, but I got tired of digging, so it was actually only a couple of feet deep. I filled the hole with sandstone boulders, then laid a couple of pieces of runway matting across the top. Next, I rigged a valve to let water from the five-gallon drum on top of the platform run down in a kind of spray. Beneath that and off to the side a foot or so was a fifty-five-gallon drum of water.

The military used hand pumps operated by a crank to pump gasoline. But after it had been used for a certain length of time, a pump became too worn to be used for gasoline. I obtained one of these old pumps and got permission to use it to pump water up to the elevated five-gallon drum. Then I made a deal with the water supply people to come by and fill the fifty-five-gallon drum. Heating it was too much trouble, so we just had cold showers. If we really wanted hot water, we could heat a helmetful, wash up, and then take a cold shower to rinse off. This shower worked pretty well, and I used it for quite a while until the weather got colder.

When we arrived in Italy, all the tents were militarily random; that is, they were dispersed so that they presented less of a target for an enemy strafing attack. In October, I went off to rest camp, where we went for a break after a certain number of missions. When I came back, all the tents had been placed in line. We had a company street with all the tent doors opening onto each side of it. This was a neat and orderly camp—and my shower was nowhere in evidence. It had been torn down. I accepted this as just another demand of the war.

We could buy eggs by the dozen from the little Italian errand boy, so sometimes I boiled eggs for afternoon or late-night snacks. Someone showed me how to dig a hole in the ground, insert a quart-sized can from the kitchen garbage, and add gasoline to it. Our helmet would hold a dozen eggs with a little water added, so we set this over the can of gasoline, lit a match, and jumped back.

I spilled some gasoline on my clothes once without realizing it. I lit the flame and left the eggs to cook. When I came back, the gas was just about burned out. I began testing to see if the eggs were done, but the gas hadn't all evaporated from my clothes, and they caught on fire. I was left with permanent burn scars on my legs, but the accident kept me from flying for only one day. I bandaged my wounds and forgot about them.

As the weather grew colder, we needed heat for our tents. The EMs down on the line provided each tent with a stove made from a five-gallon oil drum. They cut a little square in the side of each can and wired a door onto it so it could be opened or closed for oxygen control. Then they cut a hole in the top for a three-inch stovepipe, and a metal section with a hole for the extension of the stovepipe was added to the top opening of each tent. This, along with sheet metal wrapped around the main tent pole, was meant to keep the heated pipe from causing a fire. Of course, in case of rain, the tent flap at the top was tied underneath the metal so that rainwater remained outside the tent.

Our stove operated on one-hundred-octane aviation gasoline. We had a tank of it, fifty-five gallons, right outside our tent, sitting up on a platform. A steel or copper pipe salvaged from wrecked airplanes, along with rubber tubing for bends and valves, served as a siphon pipe. We ran the pipe underneath the floor of the tent and brought it over to the stove and up into the side of it. The pipe ended in more than two inches of sand that sat in the bottom of the stove. When we wanted heat, we would open the valve to let some gas into the sand, adjust the flow so that only a drop of gas came in at a time, and then we would light the sand with a match. The gasoline burned slowly because it was in the sand, so we had the fire and heat under control. We could trust it, to a limited extent.

I got my nickname, Fox, while setting up a stove for the squadron flight surgeon. To start the siphon, I was sucking on the gas tubing connected to the fifty-five-gallon tank outside his shack when I told him to "run outside quick like a fox" and clamp off the fuel line. When he came back inside, he said, "I'm going to call you Fox from now on," and he did. That stove never exploded or gave anyone any trouble, and the nickname stuck even years later in peacetime.

We had cold and snow and rain that winter in Ramitelli. I don't remember whether we left the tent fire going at night or not. Occasionally a stove fire would get out of control, but not very often. There was absolutely no saving a tent once it caught fire, because of the constant source of one-hundred-octane gasoline. For some unknown reason, only enlisted personnel's tents, none of our officers' tents, ever burned because of a stove fire. The guys were lucky to get out with their lives. There were fire extinguishers, great big drums of carbon dioxide mounted on wheels so they could be moved quickly in case there was a fire, but nobody was able to put out a fire in time to save that first tent. If they were lucky, they prevented any neighboring tents from catching fire.

Wise-ass Martin got into trouble once because of his creative use of the available carbon dioxide. You see, one of the things we got in our PX ration was beer. How do you cool beer? Easy. You take your barracks bag and wet it down with water, place the beer inside it, and then take the fire extinguisher and turn it on full blast inside the wet bag. Carbon dioxide under pressure comes out and forms snow, and there it is on your beer. Let it sit for a little while, and you've got cold beer.

First I would get a notion, such as how to cool my beer. Then somebody else would get wind of it. The next thing I knew, someone had overdone it, or done it wrong, and then there was always trouble. The skipper gave us a big lecture on wasting carbon dioxide. It was put there to save lives and equipment, and here we were cooling beer with it. The guys had to go down to Bari or some damn place like that to get those tanks charged again, and there was no more cold beer.

I like to think that the 100th Squadron had a good mess. We had a wooden building. The floor stood about a foot above grade so it could stay dry. The sides went up about four feet, and above that was screen. We could stand up inside without any problem. The roof must have extended to provide shade and shelter from the rain, because it never seemed uncomfortable. I don't remember where the stove was, but I do not recall ever being cold.

We ate from tin plates and cups and had cutlery without having to use our GI mess kits. The tables were sturdy, and we sat on benches like the ones on picnic tables in a park. Lieutenant Banks, the mess officer, and his men knew how to bargain with the Italians to get eggs and a few other things from them. I, too, bought eggs, as I've said, but what came as a surprise were the watermelons available when they were in season. The fact that the grass and the watermelons in Italy and in Africa were just as green as in America was a revelation for me.

The mess breakfast was good. The eggs were sometimes fresh, sometimes scrambled or powdered, and with them came Spam, bread, coffee, and maybe jam. It seemed to me that if I had to go out and get killed (which I believed would never happen), I wouldn't go hungry on that last mission. Everything was new to me, a replacement pilot just getting established, but I did not hear the constant complaints about army food that I had heard back in the States. People ate what was served, three hot meals a day, and it was no "bird shit on a shingle" (creamed hamburger on toast). Besides, a pilot wasn't going to get anything else to eat for six or seven hours until he returned from a mission, so we ate up.

When we did return, the beautiful Red Cross girls greeted us with happy, winning smiles. They served doughnuts and lemonade or coffee at the debriefing, which was the reporting of the mission's actual events to intelligence officers. Unlike briefings, debriefings could be held in the open air rather than in a secure area such as the operations building.

I have no specific memory of meals on days when I was not flying except for the Thanksgiving Day dinner. The army special ration for that day included turkey, stuffing, sweet potatoes, cranberry jelly, some other vegetables, pumpkin pie, and Chianti. I ate until I was stuffed, drank some more Chianti, and ate some more. That was the finest meal served to me in my three plus years in the service. Looking back, I wonder how the army got that much turkey to that many people for one special day's meal. It was a quartermaster miracle!

CHAPTER 6

I AM IN THE WAR!

Whenever I was assigned to a combat mission, I was usually notified the day before, around the time of the evening mess. That meant I would not be spending much time at the officers' club that evening. There I could have indulged in non-American liquors mixed with juice, lemon or nonstandard grapefruit, but incurring a hangover or headache was not the way I wanted to prepare for a mission. I didn't need a courage boost.

On the morning of a mission, I would be awakened by one of the squadron officers, often the assistant operations officer assigned to the duty. If either of my tentmates was scheduled to fly the mission, he, too, was awakened; if not, he slept through my rousing. I got out of my sleeping bag, turned on the electric light, folded my mosquito netting on the frame, straightened my bed, washed, and shaved.

I dressed in long underwear if the weather was cold enough and donned an olive drab uniform—either summer or winter weight, depending on the season. Then I put on my wool flying suit and slipped fur-lined flying boots over my GI shoes. My muddy, cruddy GI flying boots were hardly in the same league as those worn by fellow pilot Captain Woodrow "Woody" Crocket. He had secured his from a British unit, and they were polished no matter the weather, but mine did the job of keeping my feet warm at thirty thousand feet.

I put my fifty-mission flighter on my head—the cap flying officers were allowed to wear during the war instead of the stiff, very formal, officers' cap. This one was much lighter in weight and softer, with a wire to make it stand out perfectly round. When one takes the wire out, it starts to droop a little.

They began to call this cap the fifty-mission flighter because fifty missions was a standard tour of duty. I carried mine all the time on missions, inside my jacket if not on my head. As I finished suiting up, I donned a leather flight jacket and stuffed the pockets with chocolate candy, Camel cigarettes, and a Zippo lighter. I grabbed my .45-caliber automatic for my shoulder holster, my bayonet, and flying gloves. I also had my "citizen ID" photos.

"Citizen ID" photo.

Someone decided that if ever we were shot down in German-occupied territory, we would stand a better chance of avoiding imprisonment if we could pass ourselves off as a citizen of that country—a laborer of some sort. So they lined us up for photographs, one after the other, each of us dressed in the same shirt, tie, and jacket. If my plane went down during combat and I was captured right away, I was in flying uniform anyway. But if I could escape and go into a forest or a small town where somebody would help me, I would have photos that my rescuers could use to create papers for me in an effort to fool the Germans into thinking I wasn't the American soldier they were looking for.

A lighted Camel in my lips, I was off to the mess hall, then the mission briefing, where a huge map of Northern and Southern Europe was uncovered. A red string ran across the map; one end was at our base, and the far end was the target. Were we headed for a dangerous strafing assignment or a rendezvous mission with an extra-long flight to Brux, Czechoslovakia, or Ploiesti, Romania? The orders commenced. We were informed of the target, our group leader, the bomb group for whom we would provide air cover, the number of B-17 or B-24 bombers in the mission, the weather conditions, the amount of antiaircraft flak, or ack-ack, expected to be in the target area, and areas to avoid flying over during approach or return from the target. There were always 50 percent more antiaircraft guns than intelligence reported. We laughed to ourselves about this. It was not as though intelligence would be there to count the guns! We were also informed as to the expected number of enemy fighter aircraft that would be near the target area, trying to intercept the bombers. We were told about supposedly safe areas that we could attempt to reach in the event of trouble and the name of the underground forces in operation there.

We were given the takeoff time and start engine time; the mission leader, lead squadron, and positions of the other squadrons; the rendezvous time with the bombers and rendezvous altitude; the radio call sign for communication with the bombers; the course the bombers would fly after rendezvous to reach their initial point (IP), the place where they would begin their bombing run; the planned time over target; the course away from the target area; the withdrawal escort time required to reach a moderately safe distance from possible enemy attack; the course back to our base; and the approximate time length of the mission from start to finish.

The last order was "Synchronize watches … Hack!" We set our watches to the appointed time and turned them off. Then, when the officer said, "Hack," we pushed the button down, and everybody's watch was supposed to start at the same time. If we could all fly at the same speed in a certain direction, or heading, based on a 360-degree compass heading setup, then we all should have been able to leave point A and arrive at point B at the same time, then turn on a different heading, and still arrive at the appointed place and time to meet the bombers we were protecting. It worked pretty well, but not exactly. If our speed differed a little, if we didn't set ourselves exactly on the course we were given to fly, or if the wind was a bit stronger than expected—if we were told there would be a 30 mph wind out of the northwest, for example, and it turned out to be a 40 mph wind out of the north-northwest—then we wouldn't arrive at point B as exactly calculated. So, when it came to arrival at point C, we would be a bit off. But if we met our bomber formation at the time our briefing officers calculated we were supposed to meet them, this was a feather in their cap.

With a bomber stream so many miles long and so many miles wide, and the fighter stream traveling at a different speed and direction coming to meet them, we saw each other before we joined up. At first we would see only a bunch of flashes above the horizon, but we knew this would be the bombers. We were looking for them, and they were looking for us, so it worked.

The amount of secret information supplied at a briefing was tremendous—the planning, the timing—but our calculated losses were never mentioned. The prevention of bomber losses to enemy fighters was paramount. I often wondered how much of this information could be picked up by the Nazis. After the fighter group leader radioed, "On course" and later, perhaps a plane in distress or a spare flyer radioed for "sack time," enemy monitoring of such radio transmissions for signal strength and direction could confirm our course direction and rate of travel. But somehow the whole operation worked in spite of the danger.

I wrote the takeoff time, our course heading out, our return course heading, and the scheduled rendezvous time with the bombers on the palm of my hand in ink so I could wash or lick it off in case of a bailout or capture. The other directions and times would take care of themselves.

The 332nd Fighter Group flew together. By now it was comprised of four squadrons: the 99th, 100th, 301st, and 302nd Fighter Squadrons. Other groups might well have been on the same mission protecting the same bombers, but they flew independently of us. Four flights of four planes each, plus a couple of spares, flew from each squadron of the 332nd. The 100th Squadron had the call sign Counter. The fourth, or D, flight in the squadron was designated Blue. After starting out in the second position to gain experience, I often flew the fourth position in the fourth flight, the D-4 position, so that made me Counter Blue Four—likely the most vulnerable position of all and not one for less-experienced pilots. After filling the fourth position for a while, one worked one's way up to position three to lead an element; and finally, when one got good enough with that, one could lead a flight.

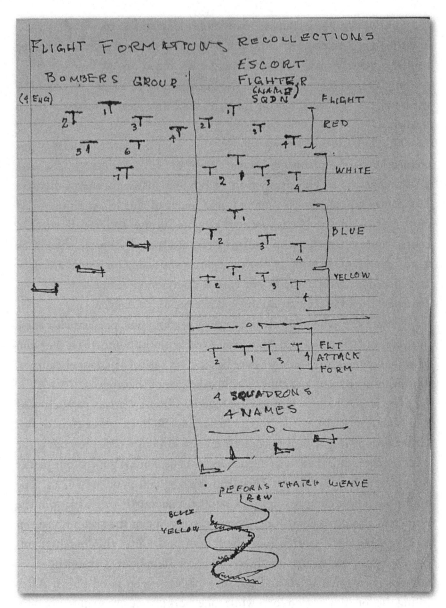

Flight formations, as I can recall them.

Flight D. I am in the front row on the right.

Originally, everyone assumed that the bombers would be able to defend themselves. When the Germans sent up fighter planes to shoot them down, the Allies quickly determined that they needed fighter escorts to make sure, as much as possible, that the bombers reached their targets. Colonel Davis, our commanding officer, provided us with this tactical order of business: chase the German fighter planes away, then come back and protect the bombers against another possible attack. "We don't want you guys to be aces," he told us. "We want you to protect the bombers."

The bombers would take off from fields a great distance away. We would take off much later and meet them at some point just before they reached the area where the Germans might intercept them. Then the fighters and bombers would fly together to the target area. Our job was to see the German fighters and dive into them before they reached the bombers. We would drop our external fuel tanks and start the dogfight before the enemy fighters could attack the bombers, turning them away. After they had left, we would return to formation, flying above the bombers to fend off attacks from the next group of fighters sent in to shoot down any unescorted bombers.

We also stayed to protect the bombers after they had dropped their loads. By then, some of the bombers would have one or more crippled engines, or they might be on fire or shot up. These stragglers were easy prey for the German fighters who were sent to shoot them down after they had emerged from the field of ground fire, and General Ira C. Eaker, commander-in-chief of the Mediterranean Allied Twelfth and Fifteenth Air Forces, wanted his bombers brought home. The return escort was much shorter because, having dropped their loads, the bombers were lighter and could fly faster. We could cover three hundred miles or more in about an hour and a half on the return trip. We didn't have to escort the bombers all the way home, but only a few hundred miles, because the German fighters chased them only so far. Once we could determine that the bombers were safe, we went our separate ways. Our presence alone helped deter attacks and increased the confidence of the bomber crews even though a lot of fighter pilots, myself included, never got the chance to actually shoot at an enemy plane during these missions.

Most of our work was escorting bombers, but sometimes our whole group was sent out to shoot up airdromes identified by Allied photo reconnaissance planes. They would spot an unusual number of planes on the ground somewhere in Europe. These planes could have been parked because they were low on fuel, or they could have been massing for a major operation, but either way, the Allies wanted them destroyed. We would get an order to fly, say, three hundred miles to an airfield, shoot up the planes on the ground there, and come back home.

Even our strafing assignments, however, were not the same as those that won the 99th its notoriety. Strafing undefended targets of opportunity near the front lines, as they did—shooting up a convoy, a gun position, or maybe the front lines themselves—while of course subject to the whims of war, was not as dangerous a proposition as strafing defended targets. When we were flying against defended areas—"through the box," as we say—we risked losing people.

Shooting at an individual airplane is generally a waste of time. The shooter has to aim at a spot ahead of the plane where he calculates that his bullet will meet it, given the travel time and trajectory of both the plane and the bullet. Instead, it is more effective for shooters to shoot into an area of sky that amounts to a box, and whatever flies through this space might get hit. We knew that and so did the Germans. Defended targets were risky.

Besides the occasional long-range strafing run and our main missions of escorting bombers, we would sometimes escort photo reconnaissance planes. An aircraft like the British Mosquito or the American P-38 would have been stripped of all its guns and armor so it could be filled with cameras. Despite the superior maneuverability of these planes, they were still vulnerable while the pilot took photos, unarmed, over enemy territory. Three to six P-51s would escort one photo reconnaissance plane to get him back to safety.

The estimated length of a mission alerted me to how closely to watch my fuel consumption. Knowledge of the capacity of the fuel tanks left me with little worry unless we got into action with enemy planes.

The return course to Ramitelli Air Base was given as a general direction toward the Adriatic Sea. The Adriatic is a big target. Allied Forces had emergency airfields at Vis and Zadar on the east side of the Adriatic and radio direction to help reach them. We also had emergency fields both north and south of Ramitelli on the west side of the Adriatic, where one needed only visual location of an airfield or a beach. We never flew at night, but in times of a solid overcast or low clouds, flying the shoreline gave us a route to Gallon Tower, our home field.

After the preflight briefing, we stopped by the group operations building to pick up our equipment—parachutes, helmets, oxygen masks, and Mae West life preservers (so named because, once inflated, they resembled the buxom figure of that popular film star). Then we were transported to the flight line. The 100th Squadron happened to be the one farthest from the operations building. We each placed our equipment into the cockpit of our aircraft under the watchful eye of our crew chief and then headed for the latrines, as personal hygiene was now in order. A pilot needed to void his intestines to help eliminate the possibility of gas at high altitude—which could have caused real physical distress—and to help avoid infection in case of a wound.

Not having a full bladder was certainly in one's favor. Each plane had a relief apparatus consisting of a funnel with a flexible tube that led to the outside of the plane. I tried using it once. I was flying at an altitude of twenty thousand feet. The outside air temperature was forty-five degrees below zero. I used the apparatus, and the liquid froze in the tubing. Later, after it thawed, that liquid flowed right back into my lap. Experience does wonders; we learned to control ourselves for more than six hours at a stretch. I completed only one mission in stinking, wet clothing.

As start-engine time approached, I put on my gear, smoked one last cigarette, and got strapped into the cockpit. I made only a cursory outside check of the plane. My crew chief, Sergeant Johnson, told me our plane was ready to go. In a way, this was really *his* plane. I was only borrowing it for this mission—a point he emphasized each time with the instruction, "Be sure to bring back my plane."

My crew chief, Roland Johnson, and me in front of our plane, Queen Cole/Sweet Eleanor.

Another view of Queen Cole, wrapped up for the night.

Before starting the engine, I checked the controls, including the ailerons, the tail rudder, and the elevators, for ease of movement. A battery big enough to start this 1,600 hp engine was too big to carry in the plane. We could take on that weight in gasoline instead and leave the battery at home. So, at startup time, the battery cart was plugged in and I began the "Clear! Switch On! Contact!" sequence.

That beautiful Rolls-Royce Merlin engine roared to life, first shaking the sleep out of itself, then settling into a throaty purr. Instruments had to be checked. Oil pressure, green. Manifold pressure, okay. Engine rpm, okay. Fuel tank selector valve checked in all five positions and set on "fuselage" for takeoff. Oxygen flow meter, checked. Artificial horizon, set. Gun heater and gun camera switches, on. Gun switches, off! I didn't have a written list, but I had memorized my start-up routine.

On signal, all planes nosed out of the hardstands with the crew chief sitting on the wing. Then we swung into line, noses angled toward the taxi strip. There we sat, waiting for the signal to move to the end of the runway for takeoff. Two other squadrons, the 301st and the 302nd, got the flare signal ahead of us. Their planes, one after another, passed in front of us going down the runway, taking off east, downhill and into the wind. After the last plane of those two squadrons had cleared the end of the runway, my squadron, the 100th Counter Squadron, would take off to the west, uphill and downwind. When we got the signal, the downward flash of the starter's arm, we, too, pulled onto the runway one at a time and took off.

I moved into position in my turn and quickly and smoothly advanced the throttle until the manifold pressure dials read 61 inches of mercury and 3,100 rpm. Fuel mixture was "full rich." These steps were performed while lining up with the runway. About a third of the way down the runway, the tail came up and the plane began to feel light on the controls. *Patience*, I told myself. *Hold the nose down a little longer; gain a little more speed.*

Me with my headset.

I didn't take time to read the airspeed indicator. The plane wanted to fly; I could feel it. *Add a little pressure back on the stick.* Rolling uphill and downwind caused me to use a little more runway and burn a little more fuel at three gallons per minute (gpm). But this P-51C (Peter-dash-five-one), my *Queen Cole*, would get me into the air with no problem whatsoever.

It took a combination of actions to get seventy-two planes started, lined up, off the runway, and airborne in minimum time. Thirty-six planes in single file took off from one end of the runway, after which thirty-six planes took off from the other end, pointed in the other direction. The entire routine took about twelve minutes—a smooth clockwork for war. Because flying time was measured by hours of fuel available, efficiency was critical.

My airplane carried more than four hundred gallons of gas. There were eighteen planes in our squadron: four four-plane flights and two spares. That means we needed seventy-two hundred gallons of gas for one squadron to fly a mission. We had four squadrons, so twenty-eight thousand eight hundred gallons of gasoline were needed for our fighter group to fly one mission. A P-51 fighter pilot was trained to be conscious of his fuel supply at all times because that just might make the difference between making it home or not.

I broke ground, and the ground noise dissolved. A firm pull on the landing gear lever retracted the wheels. I checked the altimeter, located the other planes, and checked the air speed. About one hundred feet up, continually climbing, I slid to the right to get out of the turbulence from the plane ahead of me. I throttled back to 2,400 rpm and thirty inches of manifold pressure, and my fuel consumption rate dropped to 1 gpm. I was still climbing.

At about fifty-four hundred feet, I slid in close to assume my formation position, which, as mentioned previously, was usually Counter Blue Four. The flight moved into group formation position, and I synchronized my propeller with my leader's. By flying directly behind the leader, I got the illusion that my propeller was standing still. This visual cue meant that my engine rpm matched his rpm with the same approximate power setting. Then I checked my instruments to be sure all were in the green.

I changed my fuel mixture control from full rich to "auto-lean" and switched from the fuselage tank to the left internal gas tank. This would use enough gas to give the bleeder system on the carburetor room to siphon and transfer a bit of gas to the left internal tank. Over the course of a four-hour flight, the bleeder moved about thirty gallons. That extra fuel gave the pilot an additional thirty minutes of flying time to get back home. Normally our missions were four and a half, maybe five, hours long, but trips to the Ploiesti oil fields or to southern France or Athens, Greece, took maybe six and a half hours. This was when we were more likely to need those magical get-me-home gallons stored by the bleeder system. When we needed it, that extra gas in the left internal tank was a lifesaver.

I checked my watch for its quarter-hour position and began timing my fuel consumption. Every half hour, I switched tanks. After using the left internal tank during the first half hour, I switched to the right external tank, then the left external. I would use up the external tanks first because they would have to be jettisoned before combat engagement. Switching between the right and left tanks helped keep the plane balanced. Then, once the external tanks were emptied, I would use the right internal tank and switch with the left internal tank every half hour until they, too, had emptied. After that I would employ the fuselage tank again. Operating from the fuselage tank also benefited aerobatic balance during combat performance.

The tank-switching procedure might seem boring to most, but not to the pilot. His life might depend on having enough fuel to reach home after an extended operation at full throttle and rich fuel mixture. In addition to checking his watch for fuel tank switching, however, he also had to be sure to fly in formation, check the positions of the three other planes in the flight, and look out for enemy fighter planes, all the while remaining as alert as possible, ready for action.

Say you are on a particular mission that has grown long. It has been busy. This is not your first mission. You are not tired, but how many times have you switched tanks? You have forgotten. The instrument needles are all in the green. The engine is purring beautifully. You know it can run ten hours or more with enough fuel.

Suddenly there is the loudest silence you have ever heard. The purr is gone. You are at twenty-six thousand feet somewhere over enemy territory. You and your plane are dropping behind. The group has left you. Is it time to panic? No! You have been trained. You realize a tank has run dry, and without so much as thinking, you reach down and switch to a good tank in one fluid motion. Pavlov's dog could not have reacted better. With a slight cough, the engine roars back to full power. You pull back into formation and immediately go back into a full head swivel, looking, protecting, and feeling slightly stupid. It may happen again on another flight, or it may never happen again, but a pilot will never forget that moment of the loudest silence in the world.

At about two thousand feet in altitude, the group assembled into its "on-course" formation, confirmed over the radio by the group leader, and it was time to relax. At this time, we were nowhere near enemy territory. We were flying northwesterly up the center of the Adriatic Sea. I slid out to a looser formation position.

It got awfully cold up there. Besides the protection of all the wool layers of clothing, we had a cockpit heater, and the sun generally helped warm things up. We each also had a leather flying jacket, although this was not the fur jacket worn by the bomber pilots. We wore our oxygen masks on takeoff for protection in case of fire, but once safely off the ground, we could take the masks off, light up a cigarette, and smoke. I opened the flare-gun port of the cockpit for fresh air. Flipping off my oxygen mask, I got out my Zippo and lit up a Camel.

After a steady climb, at twelve thousand feet we were still in fairly safe territory, but now it was time to go to work. I released the cigarette to be sucked out the flare-gun port and closed the port. We never carried flares, by the way. The flare gun was there, but for cockpit safety, we were told, we had no flares. I checked my cockpit heater, strapped on my oxygen mask, checked its control indicator, and began scanning the skies for bogies— enemy fighters. I'd seen some at a distance during previous missions, but never close by. Would this be the day?

We had been climbing for more than an hour and a half at 180 mph, combing the sky the entire time with our necks swiveling 360 degrees, looking for any sign of enemy fighter activity. Any dust speck on the horizon in any direction, high or low, we looked at six times to discern any possibility of its being a bogie—a Messerschmitt Bf 109 or any other fighter plane of the German Luftwaffe. The sky was clear, light blue from horizon to horizon, with only a few flat swatches of clouds off to our left. The sun was bright, warming me on the little exposed sliver of skin between my helmet, goggles, and oxygen mask. I glanced at the external thermometer, which read sixty-seven degrees below zero. *It's cold out there, baby!*

The only way I found to avoid being hungry on a long mission was to enjoy a thick, hard chocolate bar, which was part of a GI meal package. I broke my bars into medium-sized chunks. Even while flying on oxygen at twenty-five thousand feet, I did not consider it dangerous to slip a chunk of chocolate under the side of my oxygen mask and into my mouth. I would then check my mask and carry on with the mission. I suppose it was not surprising that I could never get anyone to trade their chocolate to me; everyone else must have been doing the same thing. Of course, this snacking would never happen during combat action, but in the calmer, more boring section of a mission—with no bogies called in, no huge cloud of smoke from flak ahead or behind, no large cities in view, or maybe with the bombers headed home—that's when I had my shot of caffeine.

About fifteen minutes before the expected rendezvous time with the bombers, an eagle eye in the group called on the radio, "Bogies, two o'clock level." I looked immediately in that direction and saw hundreds of silver flashes of light in a narrow band just above the horizon. We were seeing a group of about 125 bombers, twenty-five to forty miles away. Were they ours? Were they some other group, and not Germans? The individual planes were not identifiable yet. The flashes occurred because it was impossible for each aircraft to fly straight and level in the turbulence created by more than four hundred engines with more than one hundred pilots at the controls, each aircraft mushing along in the thin air found at twenty-five thousand feet.

Our group leader made the prescribed radio call on channel A to identify us with the bomber group we were to escort. I didn't hear that transmission because I was on channel C, listening to my squadron's commands. We continued on course but climbed about five thousand feet higher than the bombers. Drawing closer, we recognized the bomber group in their B-24s with the big green tails.

Now nerves began to tighten up. I checked my oxygen, turned my gun switches on, and switched my gas consumption to an internal tank. Our group broke into its four squadrons. Two squadrons flew on either side of the pattern and level to guard against attacks from below. Two were assigned as high squadrons and started flying back and forth three thousand to five thousand feet above the bombers in what's called the zig-zag thatch weave pattern. This maneuver placed them in a position to see and intercept any Germans who attacked at any angle from above. German fighter aircraft generally flew higher than we did so they could dive down toward our bombers.

Ahead, on the horizon, was a gray smudge of smoke. It grew blacker as we approached. This was the product of ack-ack from the guns of German ground forces. Their guns were positioned before and surrounding the target area, firing at the air space ahead of the target. The bombers would have to fly in a straight line at whatever altitude they were supposed to bomb from, and the antiaircraft shells were set to burst at the bombers' altitude. This cloud of flack was fifteen to twenty miles long, a half mile wide, and two thousand or more feet thick in the pattern of coverage. It began a few miles before the IP and continued along the path of the bomb run and through the breakaway turn the bombers made to head home.

The whole group of bombers and escort fighters sped on toward this black cloud of death made by thousands of 88 mm shells fired from the ground to hit, damage, or destroy any plane near the point of explosion. As the bombers continued through the cloud, the fighter squadrons pulled off to the side. Seldom did German fighters fly through the bomb run defense, and of course we could do nothing against ground fire. The bomber crews knew that our squadrons would return to fly protection for them after they had finished their breakaway turn.

Believe me; you never want to be totally out of gas when you're flying over enemy territory. As the Germans retreated, we flew longer and longer missions, which meant we had to be ever more cognizant of our fuel supply, ever more careful with its use. If we didn't think we would make it back to our base before running out of fuel, we looked for any friendly nearby airfield so we could refuel.

Once, in October of 1944, just before I was due for promotion, I needed gas. I found a British Army airfield, landed, and got gasoline. Exuberant with relief at having finished a mission and found enough gas to get home—having cheated death once again—I took off, turned around, and came back down the runway just a few feet off the ground at a very high speed.

The war was still fun for me, but the British were not amused. I hadn't asked the tower for permission to buzz the runway. They sent the report of my infraction all the way up to the British Army Air Force Command, and then orders came all the way down our chain of command. Eventually they got to the commander of the 100th Fighter Squadron, Captain Andrew Turner, and he sent for me. He said, "We have this message that has come down to us, and I have my orders, which say you are to be court-martialed. Do you want to be court-martialed?" He was a very nice person. I said, "No sir." I didn't want to go through that. He said, "Well, you have to be punished."

In the end, my promotion was held up for three months. I didn't attain the rank of first lieutenant until January 4. That didn't bother me much, however. While the reprimand was tumbling down to me, I received a major token of appreciation for another action of mine.

Colonel Taylor presents me with the DFC.
Colonel Davis is in the background.

Presentation of DFC awards by
Colonel Taylor as Colonel Davis looks on.
October 6, 1944, Ramitelli.

The Distinguished Flying Cross was awarded to me on October 6, 1944. I was one of the first guys in my class to receive that honor. The mission cited occurred in early October 1944. It was a strafing run in preparation for the Allied invasion of Greece, which was still held at the time by Germany. We hit airdromes in Tatoi, Kalamaki, Eleusis, and Megara. I was awarded the DFC along with Edmund Thomas, Charles Tate, Richard Harder, Spurgeon Ellington, Clarence Dart, and a couple other men I can't recall. I had not shot down any Germans; I hadn't torn up any airplanes. I was just so eager and ready to fly that somehow or other somebody must have thought this should be commended before I got myself killed by my enthusiasm.

We had a busy schedule, but every so often we would earn a trip to our rest camp in Naples. There we could hang out at the bar or have dinner with friends. We could make sand figures on the beach, wade in the water, sail, or take an excursion boat away from the shoreline. What we could not do, as I've said before, was visit the Isle of Capri.

At a rest camp dinner in Rome, 1945: me, Nelson, Powell, Holsclaw.

Sailing during rest camp.

A fellow from my hometown, Roger Lang, was flying P-38s as a reconnaissance pilot. In Naples, or possibly Rome, he ran into friends of mine—pilots spending time at our rest camp. He stepped up to them and asked about Bob Martin, inquiring as to whether or not they knew him. When they answered in the affirmative, he said, "Tell him I said hello."

Shortly after they got the message to me, I had occasion to go to Roger's field headquarters because I had to have my picture taken for a new ID card. I asked to look up Rog but was denied. They had to keep us segregated. The only place Blacks and whites could meet in the military was on the killing field in the sky.

Near midnight on New Year's Eve, I was out celebrating with a couple of classmates. We had no missions scheduled for the next day, so yes, we were a wee bit tipsy. Someone slipped, and we all fell flat on our faces in ankle-deep mud. Then we all fell to laughing. Happy thoughts! We were happy to be alive and seeing 1945.

CHAPTER 7

MISSION TO MEMMINGEN

I don't know when I started flying number four. That is approximately number sixteen in the formation, since, as I've said before, each squadron formation had four flights of four planes each and, normally, two extra planes that were supposed to move up and take the position of any pilot in the first sixteen in his squadron that had any trouble, couldn't keep up, and had to take sack time.

A pilot started out as number two in, generally, the second flight. This is number six in the formation. He flew this position until he got accustomed to combat, showed that he could follow his leader and protect his number-five man (the leader of the second flight), and was a reliable pilot. Once a pilot had proven himself, he wound up at the back as "Tail-end Charlie"—the position most vulnerable to attack. If he happened to be at the back of the last flight of the last squadron formation, however—number sixty-four if you don't count extras—he never stayed there during the entire flight.

During World War I and the early part of World War II, when a flying unit attacked a target, many times the number-three and number-four men got killed because by the time they came through the enemy would have adjusted its range of fire so that they could hit Tail-End Charlie. They might have missed the first plane and gotten closer on the second one, and by the time the fourth plane came through, they had him zeroed. If the first planes hadn't blasted the defenders out of their position, those defenders knew how to line up on the last man.

We had a captain who flew his ship in a kind of crab pattern. He thought he was fooling the enemy. They would shoot at him and miss but get the next guy. Well, it happened once that they shot up and hit the number-three man. I was number four, and I did not get hit.

We weren't attacking anything at the time; we were heading home because this number-three man had engine trouble and could not continue the mission. We were so far over German territory that we wouldn't let him fly home by himself—not with engine trouble. It weakens the mission when an entire flight of four planes has to leave, because that removes sixteen guns that could have been shooting at the enemy. But, since no one could tell what had happened to cause the trouble, no one could do anything to help this guy except not allow him to fly home alone.

Nobody had been shot down; nobody had been killed or wounded. We were on our way home thinking we were okay, and then, *wham!* They hit this guy. His plane caught on fire, and he had to bail out over Lake Balaton in Hungary. He was captured by civilians and spent the rest of the war in a prison camp.

We strafed airfields at Athens. We accompanied bombers to Vienna, Salzburg, Munich, and Stuttgart. As the war progressed and wound down and the German forces were withdrawing, we flew farther and farther to protect the bombers, maybe over Prague, Czechia, or Budapest, Hungary, four hundred or five hundred miles away. The Allies never bombed areas near the extermination camps. We flew to southern France to strafe beaches and flew cover when bridges were bombed there. We flew to targets within about a 190° radius from Ramitelli, anywhere between Avignon, France, and Athens, Greece. The Germans were all over Europe at that point. By bombing German oil fields and refineries, particularly in Ploesti, Romania, Allied bombers were crippling the German war machine. While German factories were producing airplanes at an increased rate, the refineries were not able to supply them with enough oil and gasoline.

My first mission was over the Udine and Po Valleys on July 16, 1944. On July 18, the 332nd Fighter Group was assigned to escort B-17s on a mission to Memmingen, Germany. We climbed on a heading up the middle of the Adriatic. The bombers' target was known, but neither we nor the B-17s flew directly toward it. Our route was considered safe. There was little or no enemy air force in northeastern Italy and almost none on the Dalmatian Coast until north of Trieste.

This illusion of safety existed until the land opened onto the great Udine Plain, which extended north to the Alps. This was home to many airfields with fighter aircraft and many antiaircraft guns. The enemy's airfields, aircraft, and antiaircraft artillery were stationed both near to and far from our targets. The targets themselves could be moved by rail for defense as needed. We had been told in the briefing, of course, how many fighters to expect and how many guns were there, but we knew they were guessing. We translated those figures into "multa flak, multa fighters." Our course was plotted so that the bombers and air support flew around, rather than directly over, cities or targets whenever possible.

On this day, we were outbound toward our target, flying over the bomber formation in the thatch-weave maneuver. Our position was somewhere over northern Italy when the radio blasted my ears. "Bogies, ten o'clock high! Counter, drop tanks."

I punched the button. The external gas tanks dropped away. I rechecked to be sure I was on internal gas and then straightened up again to follow my leader, all without further orders. The split second it took to switch tanks, when my head was below cockpit level, was all it took. My leader was *gone*. I began diving, twisting, and looking, but I didn't see anybody or anything. I had not seen the bogies.

I dived at, I guess, about 400 mph. I wasn't looking at gauges. I searched for my leader. My supercharger, which allowed the engine to operate at high speeds in the low pressure of high altitudes, had cut out, unneeded, so I knew I was at about fifteen thousand feet (or fifteen "angels"), when I circled. I didn't see anyone anywhere. I was alone. Instinct told me not to stay there alone. Somebody would see me—somebody I had not seen first. I climbed back to thirty thousand feet and circled again.

A minute or so later, another Red Tail came up to my altitude. We circled and wagged wings for ID. After a few minutes, with no other aircraft approaching, we started south. We spotted a German plane flying south, trailing a long stream of white smoke. He was moving away. We couldn't catch him when we "firewalled" our planes (went full throttle). My Red Tail buddy continued on as though he still thought he could catch him, and he, too, was gone.

I flew south at thirty thousand feet toward the Adriatic. I had already dropped my external tanks and the flying time they provided. Would there be any Germans waiting for me? Would there be some super shots of ack-ack sent for me? Every so often I jinked, making sudden maneuvers to mess with the enemy radar.

When I got well out over the Adriatic, I turned southeast and began a slight dive to pick up speed, knowing this would get me back to Ramitelli faster. When I returned to the field, my crew chief greeted me, concern written across his face. What had happened to me? Was I shot up, lost, or what?

The energy at the debriefing was exuberant, but I felt like a deflated balloon in the midst of the celebration. This was the best day the 332nd had ever had. Eight of our guys had shot down eleven enemy planes in air battles over northeastern Italy and near the target. The leader of this mission, Jack Holsclaw, had shot down two Bf 109s. His wingman, Walter Palmer, had gotten one. My element leader, Clarence "Lucky" Lester, had shot down three Bf 109s from his P-51 *Miss-Pelt*, the biggest single day for any Tuskegee Airman up until then. And Edward Toppins, Charles Bailey, Lee Archer, Roger Romine, and Hugh Warner had each shot down one enemy fighter as well.[28] But I got nothin', except back.

The whims of fate can be cruel. Eight pilots got to bask in glory that day, but three never made it back. Gene Browne and Wellington Irving were shot down by enemy aircraft near the target area. Browne survived but was taken prisoner; Irving died in the crash. Oscar Hutton of the 100th Fighter Squadron was also lost that day, yet four members of the 100th earned the Distinguished Flying Cross for their actions on this mission: Lester, Holsclaw, Palmer, and Andrew Turner. Their commendation stated that the bomber formation was attacked that day by three hundred enemy fighters.

---

[28]   Bucholtz, 332nd *Fighter Group*, 53–54.

Captain Andrew "Jug" Turner, CO of the 100th Fighter Squadron (right), congratulates First Lieutenant Jack Holsclaw in front of Lester's plane, which indicates three aerial victories.

On one of the two times I found myself short on gas, I landed at an emergency field to get enough fuel to make it home. This was in early December. I was a little panicked and landed hot (too fast). I was trying to slow the plane down and turn it around with a ground loop when a wheel caught in a hole in the ground. This spun the plane and caused it to nosedive. The propeller was driven into the ground.

I should have slowed the plane before landing. Everything would have been okay if I had just made a short landing, but hindsight is always twenty-twenty. Now they would have to send a big truck up there and cut the airplane, maybe even remove the wings, to bring it back to our field. I didn't know how much damage was done to the engine or any of the internal connections when the propeller was stopped so suddenly. I had not run the plane off the end of the runway into a bunch of rocks, but it would still need a lot of work before it was flight-ready again. I was sorry for causing a loss that could have been avoided with a better choice. But I was alive. I knew things could have been worse.

So many things could, and sometimes did, go wrong. I had heard that one guy was killed because a dinghy started to inflate inside the cockpit of his plane. The dinghy, a rubber raft, was stowed in the cockpit in case a pilot ended up in the water. It was inflated by two carbon dioxide cartridges operated by a mechanism the pilot could control. But sometimes the mechanism operated accidentally and inflated the dinghy when it wasn't needed or wanted. This seemed to be the case for the pilot I heard about. He undid his safety belt, but the dinghy continued to inflate until it pushed him forward on the stick. This sent the plane into a dive from which the pilot could not regain control.

Knowing this, when on one mission I felt a strange pressure on my chest against my safety harness, I thought, "Is this happening to me?" A little while later I knew it to be true: my dinghy was inflating. But I was determined not to die like that other guy; being forewarned, I could save myself. I pulled out of formation, withdrew my standard-issue bayonet, somehow reached around behind me, and scratched through the canvas cover of the dinghy. I managed to cut deep enough into the rubber for the pressure to subside.

No fighter pilot wanted his record besmudged by an implausible explanation as to why he had returned early. There were quite a few early returnees with sometimes dubious excuses, and I did not want to be one of them. I figured that, should I get shot down over water, my Mae West would hold me up until I had used the repair kit provided to patch the holes in the dinghy and inflate it. I got back into formation and flew on with the mission. We were lucky not to face combat that day. I did not get shot down and have to bail out over water.

On another mission, we took off flying at a very low altitude because of a solid overcast. About an hour from base, we found a hole in the clouds and spiraled up to about twenty-two thousand feet. In the clear above the clouds, we leveled off and continued on course. I started to change gas tanks.

I had spent about seventy gallons of fuel at this point, so there should have been enough fuel remaining for five to six hours of continued flight, with the plane kept in trim by alternating the five tanks. But my gas cock, the mechanism that shifted the gas flow from one tank to another, was frozen. I tried and tried but could not turn the thing. This meant that, although the plane still carried about 350 gallons of fuel, once the current feeding tank ran dry, I was effectively out of gas and would have to start walking. I called for sack time and turned around. I found the same hole in the clouds, descended to the deck, and flew back to the base. They indeed found ice in my gas cock, and I was excused.

The Allied invasion of southern France occurred on August 15, 1944. Three days before the invasion, the 332nd was ordered to take out the radar on the beaches. This equipment was very heavily defended. We would lose several pilots that day, and several other pilots would be captured and sent to prison camp, including Alex Jefferson from my class, but of course we didn't know what lay ahead when we started out.

I took off with everyone else but immediately noticed gasoline streaming from my wing tank. I could see it.

The other guys in the squadron saw it too, and then I heard over the radio, "Martin, go back and get that main wing tank gas cap tightened."

I had to wait until everybody had taken off, but then I turned around and landed right away. The mechanic was waiting at the end of the runway. He jumped up on the wing, tightened the gas cap, and I turned around and took off again.

The mission was to fly at about fifteen thousand feet to the target. I had my direction. I took off after the others, but I could not find them. I kept flying and flying, first over central Italy, then over the Tyrrhenian Sea. I could see a big island that I knew to be Corsica, but I still couldn't see any fighters from my group.

Just as I had decided that there was nothing to do but take sack time and return to base, I looked down and saw more battleships, more freighters, more of any kind of boat than I had ever seen. The Allies were carrying troops and ammunition into southern France for the invasion. And there they were, right below me.

I turned off my radio, thinking, *I ain't gonna let out a peep to let them know I'm here.* Even so, as I turned, a couple of destroyers turned right with me, and I knew they would do anything to keep the invasion a surprise. I went home. I believe it saved my life that I wasn't on that mission. Lucky me.

One day we had a stand down, a chance to take a break. People in the air corps knew people in the quartermaster corps and every other branch of service overseas, and occasionally there were opportunities like this to get together. We would scout different Italian towns to learn about the food and drink available.

I was riding with some of the quartermaster officers when the military police approached and claimed we had been speeding.

Somebody in the group replied, "You MPs are stopping my guys all the time. We get more tickets on this road to Manfredonia. What's wrong with you guys?"

The MP retorted, "We were right to stop you! You've been speeding, and we've got to give you a ticket. We've got our duty to perform."

It was the pilot's turn to speak. It just so happened that I had no mission assignment the next day either and I had to slow-time an airplane. "We'll come over this road at four hundred miles an hour tomorrow," I said, "and you won't even touch us!"

Major Italian roads were generally lined with trees unless heavy fighting had taken them out, and this road was no exception. The next day, I was in the *Queen Cole*, sitting right on top of those trees, flying over the road at 400 mph. The trees stood about twenty feet high, but one little pine tree stuck up higher. I picked up my wing as I approached but still ticked it.

I put the plane on the ground, happy to be alive, and told the mechanic, "I think I hit something while I was flying kind of low ... like a tree." He later told me that he had found wood in the gun barrel but was able to remove it. The leading edge of the wing was a little dented, too, but the plane was still flying. Lucky me.

On November 21, two days before Thanksgiving, Lieutenant Roscoe Brown and I set off on a mission under the command of Captain Lawrence Dickson. The task was to provide protective cover for a photo reconnaissance plane. The target was in the area of Prague, Czechia.

A successful photo reconnaissance mission entailed piloting the photo plane both to and from the target area and making the actual photo runs free from enemy intervention. The photo pilot's defensive advantage was his extreme maneuverability—his ability to turn more sharply to avoid being hit by gunfire. He might also dive or turn into the clouds and disappear from sight.

The American photo plane, an unarmed P-38, flew faster than most propeller-driven planes, including our P-51s, but it could not match the speed of a jet. The German Luftwaffe was known to be flying jet planes by this time—the Messerschmitt 262, with a superior speed of 500 mph. The new jet fighters were reported to be operating in the Prague area, so fighter escort was all but mandatory on this mission.

This was Captain Dickson's sixty-eighth mission, a remarkable achievement. White pilots were required to fly only fifty missions to complete a tour. Black pilots had to complete seventy missions before being sent back to the United States for rest and rehabilitation (R&R). At least Dickson would easily be home for Christmas.

Captain Dickson with Nino, one of our Italian errand boys.

Dickson, Brown, and I left Ramitelli at the appointed morning hour, crossed the Adriatic in clear weather, and proceeded on course to a midair rendezvous with the "photo recce" at the specified time high over what was then Yugoslavia. From the rendezvous, our four planes flew north toward Prague.

After about an hour on course at more than 200 mph, we were still climbing to get above an extensive cloud system. The cloud height reached twenty-four thousand feet in spots and extended almost two hundred miles to the horizon in any direction. A massive weather system, a dangerous obstacle in its own right, completely covered what seemed like all of northern

Yugoslavia and Austria, with its high alpine peaks, and might have extended as far as the Prague area.

Dickson radioed that his engine seemed to be cutting out. We were at an altitude of about twenty-six thousand feet. Shortly after, he reported he was keeping his engine running by hand-pumping the engine primer pump. This was an emergency procedure. He was losing power and speed. Because Brown and I were flying on his wings, the three of us were unable to keep up with the P-38 photo plane.

Dickson led us north. Eventually we found a hole in the clouds that was maybe twenty miles in diameter. We gradually let down, and about the time we reached twenty thousand feet, Dickson told us his engine was running properly.

At this point, we had not only lost visual contact with the photo plane but were also so far behind it that it was clear to me we were facing an aborted mission. Without orders to do otherwise, the course of action was to remain with, and escort to safety, the crippled aircraft. We had to hope that the photo plane pilot, with his maneuverability and some luck, might evade a jet attack, photograph his target, and return home safely.

We began climbing out of the hole and turned to head south. Dickson continued to climb above the cloud formation in an apparent attempt to avoid flying through clouds on instruments with an untrustworthy engine. Once again at twenty-six thousand feet, and only about two thousand feet above the clouds, he reported his engine cutting out as before. He was forced again to hand-operate the priming pump. Performing this operation twice for about twenty minutes or so must have been very tiring. He must have decided he couldn't continue. In such a predicament, the best a pilot can do is to find someplace to land or bail out. His last hope was to be captured and protected by German soldiers. It was better to end up as a prisoner of war than to be killed by angry civilians.

From a few thousand feet above the clouds, we began a gradual descent, looking for a hole in the clouds, and luck was with us. We came to an opening about twenty-five miles wide where we could look down. We spotted a broad, snow-covered valley with a line of mountains on both sides running northeasterly. As Dickson led us down into this valley, he must have been facing serious trouble. Even at this lower altitude, he did not radio to say that his engine was running properly.

Now we were approaching a town, which I guessed might be Klagenfurt, Austria. It was a town roughly along our flight path. We were flying in clear air, surrounded by what seemed like a tunnel of white. Below us, the valley was covered with late November snow. The mountain walls on either side were the same harsh white except for a narrow black band near their tops. There the mountains disappeared into the dense white clouds that formed the roof of the tunnel. Only the dull red spires of a few scattered rooftops in the rapidly nearing town provided a rare glimpse of color.

Here we were, flying over a scene that might have been picture-postcard pretty had the whiteness not been bitterly cold and within enemy territory. When, and from where, would the bursts of antiaircraft fire come? Were we getting too close to the town to avoid getting hit? It seemed to me that Dickson must take some decisive action before we got there. This was the time to start praying for a miracle.

My hope for his safety rose when he jettisoned his cockpit canopy. This action indicated that he was preparing to leave his crippled fighter rather than attempt a disastrous landing on unknown, snow-covered, mountainous terrain. I moved out farther to the side. I wanted to get a better view and avoid his plane, because without anyone at the controls, it could turn in any direction.

During the second or two it took me to slide out, Dickson just disappeared. Lacking power, his plane lost speed. He dropped behind and below me so quickly that he and his aircraft were immediately lost to view. I didn't know whether Dickson had actually bailed out. I didn't know whether his parachute had opened and he was floating downward or whether he was still with his plane.

I turned to reverse my course, as did Brown from the opposite side. We looked for any kind of evidence: a parachute, wreckage, a burning plane, a column of smoke. We continued searching, desperately hoping to see some sign of Dickson in that part of the valley, but we saw only snow.

Now the senior officer, I finally called off the search and led Brown back to the hole, where we climbed above the clouds and set a course south toward the Adriatic. After a few minutes on course, Brown radioed, "Do you think he's okay, Martin?" I replied, "I hope so." There was silence. Then Brown asked, "Can we go back for another look?"

The odds of us finding Dickson were then no better unless in the meantime the plane wreckage had caught on fire or he somehow made a signal. I turned and led us back to the hole. We descended into the valley and steered toward the town, hunting, once more searching that unyielding whiteness.

I didn't have a flare pistol. Instead I fired a few short bursts from my guns as we neared the town in an attempt to alert someone that a rescue was needed. Still there was no visible evidence indicating that a plane had landed, crashed, or caught fire. If Dickson and his plane were down there, they were either lost deep in the snow or had been found and he was now in the hands of the enemy.

I led us back to the hole. We climbed again to clear the clouds and headed south toward Ramitelli. About an hour later, I figured we should be somewhere over the Adriatic Sea—where, I wasn't sure, but the expanse of clouds indicated that the entire weather system had continuously moved south as we had operated above it. A hole in the clouds gave us a glimpse of open blue water far below us, and we spiraled down, almost to the surface. The bottoms of the clouds were less than a thousand feet above the water, and there were patches of rain.

We flew southwest to locate the shoreline of Italy, and at an altitude of about four hundred feet, we traced the coastline. At Ramitelli, the cloud base was at seven hundred feet. We landed without further incident. The squadron intelligence officer heard our report and asked a few questions. The interrogation was finished. We never saw Captain Dickson alive again.

Captain Lawrence E. Dickson gave his life in the service of his country while trying to complete a combat mission in late 1944. Lieutenant Brown and I regretted the loss of a comrade and a fine pilot. We regretted the circumstances in which we, his wingmen, ultimately could be of no help.

I was able to be of assistance when I participated in a special mission toward the end of the war. As the Soviets advanced on Romania and Hungary, both of which had joined the Axis alliance, it was obvious that Hitler's power was breaking. Authorities there knew that they had limited options. They could kill their prisoners of war, around two thousand downed Allied airmen, before the Soviets got to them. They could go to the expense of feeding and transporting these men, using resources they really did not have. Or they could curry favor with the Allies by offering to return these prisoners if Allied forces could pick them up. They decided to let the Allies come and pick them up.

Speed in evacuation was critical; I believe only one trip was made. Bomber groups removed the guns, ammunition, and bombs from their planes and flew to a field where the prisoners had been assembled from various locations. I would say there were about a hundred bombers, B-17s and B-24s. Without all the armament, each bomber could hold about twenty men. This was just enough of a major operation that no bombing was carried out that day.

We fighter pilots arrived at the appointed place and circled overhead, prepared to shoot up any interference. No German fighter planes came to interfere, however, so the bombers landed and loaded without incident. We escorted them to safety in Italy, and from there, those two thousand freed pilots were able to return home.

CHAPTER 8

SHOT DOWN OVER YUGOSLAVIA

There is an air corps rule best remembered from day one: never volunteer! My squadron had another rule too, though it was an unwritten code never spoken, to my knowledge, until I said it myself on this particular morning: a new pilot should not be sent on a strafing mission until he has completed five escort missions. By the time he reached this milestone, he would have earned an Air Medal and would know his way home. How the rule came to be, I don't really know. I never knew who had followed it on my behalf, but somewhere in squadron history there is a pilot who stood in for Martin once, maybe twice.

For some reason on the morning of March 3, 1945, I attended a mission briefing in our operations tent even though I was not scheduled to fly, and I learned about the strafing mission planned for that day. Afterward, I looked over the roster and, seeing the names of some pilots who had just joined the squadron, volunteered to take the place of one of them. Lieutenant Alphonso Simmons volunteered as well. Captain Mattison approved the changes without fanfare and appointed Lieutenant Simmons to lead the second section. Both Simmons and I should have been forewarned of disaster, however, having done the unthinkable: we had volunteered.

My plane, the wonderful *Queen Cole*, was a P-51C with a greenhouse canopy and four .50-caliber machine guns, but the *Queen* was not to go on this ride. Since this was a designated strafing mission, a new P-51D with a bubble-top canopy and six .50-caliber guns was volunteered for me by its regular pilot, Lieutenant Bob Williams. The extra firepower in this baby meant I could really clobber something. But there was that *V* word again.

Actually, looking back, I see that the bubble canopy probably saved my life. It would have been harder to bail out of my greenhouse canopy because it peeled open, with hinges here and hinges there. I could open it in several different places. It opened to either side, and I'd have to climb out. The bubble canopy slid back so that the whole thing was open and I could just fall out. At least that's the way it was supposed to work.

Pilots have always felt a strange connection between luck and numbers, and there was another connection I didn't make until years later. Because I was not scheduled to fly, I had spent the previous evening at the officers' club, indulging in a modest amount of drinking and gambling. A friend and I had pooled two dollars each in a blackjack game. By judiciously handling our bets, we worked the pool up until our luck disappeared and we busted out at sixty-four dollars. The mission I volunteered for after losing sixty-four dollars? It was my sixty-fourth.

Our mission this day was to fly to Maribor, a railroad junction center in what is now Slovenia. We were to strafe rail traffic from there northward and attack other targets as we had opportunity. We flew out on course at about fifteen thousand feet over a solid undercast of clouds. At our estimated time of arrival (ETA), we found a hole in the clouds and let down until we were in the clear at about six thousand feet. But we were far short of our intended target. We had been briefed to expect 50 mph headwinds and had calculated our arrival based on that level of resistance. We had actually been flying for a couple of hours against headwinds of over 100 mph, and now we were fifty miles from where we had planned to be. So we located the main rail line extending southeastward from Maribor, and the hunt was on. Once we had sighted a train, Lieutenant Roscoe Brown led the attack with eight planes; our group, led by Lieutenant Simmons, flew top cover at six thousand feet.

Shortly thereafter, we heard that Lieutenant Brown's plane had been hit by flack and that he was returning to base. Lieutenant Simmons was directed to command the squadron, and while flying in a large circle to regroup the squadron accordingly, we flew over an airfield at Zagreb, Yugoslavia (now Croatia). This field seemed to be in good condition, but it appeared to be nonoperating. There was no sign of activity, no flak— nothing. Not a wink. But we spotted two aircraft hidden under trees at the northeast corner of the field with no revetments, no protection except the trees. Simmons announced that we would get those planes. We could hit these easy targets before turning back to the railroad and get a couple of pictures in the bargain.

We flew northeast and dived in a turn to pick up speed. Then we flew back toward the airfield to make a pass headed southwest at treetop height and about 450 mph. I forgot all about the rest of the squadron. At the command "Drop tanks!" I switched to an internal gas tank and decided I would delay my drop so that I could release my tanks like bombs and perhaps start a fire in the woods or on the planes after I had strafed them. The third plane in the flight called to say he couldn't release his tanks. He turned out of the formation and I gave him no more thought. In my mind, he wasn't a member of the 100th anymore. As we approached the field, I could no longer see the planes. The one-hundred-plus-mile-per-hour wind we had faced on the flight toward Maribor was still blowing. On our turn from the east, we were blown off to the south so that we arrived at the center of the field instead of the northeast corner, where the planes were. As we came over the edge of the trees, the field just opened up like blossoms. It lit up with a thousand winking points of light from every direction, and none of them were friendly.

Simmons started a hard turn to the right. He knew better; we all knew better. You don't make a hard turn in a field of fire that intense because it slows you down, giving those bullets a better chance to find you. I never saw him again.

I continued across the field, making a slight turn to the left, and saw a machine gun nest with two men firing at me. Lined up with them, I dropped my tanks and started firing. My bullets hit the dirt far beyond them. I dropped ten degrees of flaps and, with the plane pitched over in a nose-down attitude, my bullet strikes marched back toward, but not quite to, the nest. Then my speed took over and marched them forward again. I stopped firing and continued across the field, where I shot at a small white building. That was my mistake. The minute you line up with something, you've given the enemy added time to correct his aim and get you.

Moments later, I heard a loud *whump*—there's no other way to describe it—and the plane jumped as if it had been kicked by something big, maybe a 20 mm. The engine coughed and then caught up and started running extra smoothly, quieter than it had on the run-in. I didn't understand what that meant, but I thought, *Okay, I got hit, but not bad.* I would go around and make another pass at the planes, maybe from a different direction. Unfortunately, that was not to be.

A few moments later, I noticed short tongues of flame coming from the exhaust stacks. I cleared the trees at the edge of the field and stayed at treetop level for perhaps a minute or more to get out of sight of ground observers. I was already headed south, toward home. I tried to radio Simmons to let him know I would have to take sack time. The flames grew longer, but the engine continued to run smoothly. I thought maybe the plane would hold up until I got out to the coast, where I could bail out, land in the water, and get rescued.

The flames coming from the exhaust stacks were in the shape of very colorful, long tubes like the balloons you see at a carnival sideshow—the kind a clown twists into animal shapes. The tubes of flame grew longer and longer, and in a short time they were flowing around the bubble canopy. I knew now that I would not make it back to base or to the coast in this plane. So would I allow myself to be so bedazzled by the beauty of those playful flames that I would sit and fry? Not me! I would have to bail out. Of course, the plane could have actually exploded, but that thought did not occur to me. I simply had no intention of frying. I sent out a Mayday call to inform someone, anyone, of my plans.

"I will walk in from here," I was reported to have said, but I heard no reply.[29]

I took the plane up about a thousand feet above the terrain, looked out to judge my height, and thought, *Not high enough.* I climbed another thousand feet—that would do! The flames were no longer part of the picture, if you can believe it. They just weren't in my conscious thoughts any longer.

The bail-out procedure was to disconnect the radio, disconnect oxygen, jettison the canopy, roll the plane onto its back, unhook the safety belt, and drop free and clear. Only it didn't work exactly like that. I unhooked the safety belt before rolling over, so I began falling out when the plane got about three-quarters rolled over. I started falling out—and suddenly got no further. My body was out, lying flat against the side of the airplane. My legs

---

[29]   Bucholtz, *332nd Fighter Group*, 101.

from the knees on down were still inside; I could not seem to get them out any further. The 300 mph airstream was holding me to the plane.

Nobody was more surprised than I that I could not just fall out, but I would not stay and fry or crash in flames! Being scared to death makes you too rigid to save your own life, and I was not about to go there. Failure was simply not in my code of thinking. What to do, then? Go back and do it right. I grabbed the edge of the cockpit and pulled myself back in, sat down, grabbed the controls, and leveled the plane. Then I did a proper quick half-roll and let go. This time I was free and clear, except that the tail was spinning toward me! Fortunately, it missed.

After finally getting clear of the plane, I counted to ten, ready to pull the ripcord. But then I perceived another problem. I had begun to wear my parachute straps loose so they would not bind and hurt or cut off circulation on a five-hour mission. After all, this was my sixty-fourth mission, and I didn't believe that anything could really happen to me. But now, suddenly, the looseness of the straps became the problem. A parachute is designed to have straps kind of tight so that when the shock of the chute opening comes, the straps just grab and hold you like a good, tight bear hug. When the wind opened my parachute, I knew, the force of the loose straps sliding up and catching my crotch and genitals could severely damage them or even cut them off. When I pulled the ripcord, the straps might save my life, but they might render me a soprano and divorce me from the men's club.

Just then I thought of the Caterpillar Club, the exclusive group of fliers who had parachuted to safety from damaged airplanes. If I had my parachute ripcord as proof of this event, I would be able to join them. So, both to protect myself and future generations and to save the D-ring, I wound my legs together in desperation, wrapped my arms around my body, and pulled the cord.

I came to, swinging back and forth, floating gently down with a huge white parachute canopy overhead. The chest buckle seemed to form a new pair of goggles in front of my face. I could taste blood. The buckle had hit my chin, knocked me out cold, and split my lip open on the inside. It was somehow just low enough to prevent my head from falling forward, which could have pitched me out of the parachute. Oh, it was great to be alive!

I grabbed the shroud lines and took stock of the situation. The ripcord was gone, but I was okay. I was coming down over a section of woods, but there was an open field nearby. I knew I did not want to get stuck in trees and find myself hanging in midair, so now I had to steer myself away from the trees. The parachute instructions state that if you pull on the shroud lines on one side, the parachute will move you in that direction. I pulled. Not in the instructions is that after you pull on the lines, your rate of descent will increase as though you don't even have a parachute.

The woods hurtled up at me. Scared, I quit trying to steer. I let go of the lines. I would just have to take the chance of getting tangled up in a tree. I guess my effort was just enough, though, because I missed the trees and landed about fifty feet away. Luckily, there was little wind. This was early March, and there were no leaves on the trees, but the patch of woods was dense. It stopped the wind, for which I had had no training. Bailing out was just too risky to practice, but without training on how to handle a strong wind or deflate a parachute, some pilots had parachuted to safety only to be dragged and killed by the wind.[30]

I collapsed my parachute, rolled it into a ball, and stuffed it under a bush. I had been flying south when I left the airfield after being hit; now the hazy sun was just west of south. I lit out running south, away from the Germans, toward home.

How did it feel to be a Black pilot on the ground in enemy territory? Was I scared? Believe me. In the two or three minutes between having my plane hit and my bailing out, I had perhaps flown fifteen or twenty miles, but I believed that a pilot did not want to be captured anywhere near the airfield he had been strafing. He might have killed an enemy soldier's brother or best pal, and the soldier just might decide to pay him back. I wanted to get far enough away to a place where, if captured, I would be just another prisoner of war. So I ran and ran.

---

[30] When I got back to Tuskegee, a mandatory parachute training was announced, and yes, I had to attend even though I had had the actual experience and was now out of the war. I learned what might have been useful after my bailout if I had had more wind to deal with. In the training, we lay facedown on a mat wearing parachute straps, and somebody would pull us along. It turns out that as long you are being dragged on your stomach, you can never get to your feet! So they taught us how to twist over onto our backs, do a backward somersault, land on our feet, turn around very quickly, and run after the chute, deflating it by pulling on the upper shrouds. After the gym session, we donned fatigues, went onto the airfield, and strapped into a parachute behind an airplane. They revved up the engine until the parachute started dragging us across the field, and then we could put into play what we had just learned.

I was wearing long underwear, still dry, a wool uniform, a wool flying suit, and a leather jacket. My fifty-mission flighter was missing, along with my fur-lined flying boots, which had not been laced too tightly for the long flight, but I had my standard GI over-the-ankle shoes. Sergeant Rudy Sablo, who was in charge of physical fitness at Tuskegee, had trained me pretty well. Our Monday-morning five-mile runs to get the weekend's booze sweated out of our systems were fun and got us in good condition, but we hadn't done any running since primary training. It was now a year and a half later. Even so, I ran for better than half an hour before I got tired.

About the time I needed a rest, I saw ahead of me a large pasture full of cows. What was this? There weren't supposed to be any cows here in German-held territory, and since there were, I assumed German soldiers must be guarding them. I flopped down onto my stomach, telling myself I would determine where the soldiers were and then go around some other way. Really, I was simply tired of running.

CHAPTER 9

TITO'S PARTISANS

After about half an hour, I had caught my breath, all the while resting, watching, looking, and trying to locate German guards. Nothing yet. I concluded there were no Germans nearby. I crawled under the barbed wire fence at the edge of the pasture and started making my way through the cows and across the field.

I was about halfway through the herd when a small boy who looked to be about ten years old stepped out from among a group of cows. It was a real surprise. If he'd had a gun, he could have shot me! He wore dark clothing and a brown cloth helmet with a five-pointed red star sewn onto it.

The boy looked at me, hesitated, and then burst out, "You American. Me partisan!"

This boy had called me an American! He had just included me in a whole culture from which I had felt essentially excluded in my own country. Here, the flag on my jacket meant more to him than the color of my skin. This took a moment for me to digest. Then I had to figure out how to communicate with the boy.

I did not know how much English he knew, but I considered that he might know Italian. A common supposition was that many Europeans knew two or three languages. In eight months in Italy I had learned about fifteen Italian words. So, in my best Italianese, I asked, "Dove tedeschi?" meaning, "Where are the Germans?"

The boy pointed north, back the way I'd come, with his whole arm. He said, "La!" meaning "There."

He hand-signaled me to follow him, and when I agreed, we started walking west. I had my hand on my .45 by this time, and I thought, "I've got him covered. If he leads me to the Germans, they are going to kill me; but he'll never get to lead another American into German hands."

Now I'm sorry I had those thoughts. I can only conclude that I must have been really scared. I pictured myself jogging through the woods and suddenly finding myself surrounded by six or eight Germans with rifles pointed at me. The scene never materialized, and I continued to follow the boy.

We crossed the pasture and continued heading west. After traveling a while along a path through the woods, we came to a small farmhouse in a clearing. The boy stopped. He motioned for me to wait. He may have said something too. He could speak a few words in several languages: German, Italian, and undoubtedly Slovakian or Serbian.

From the edge of the clearing, the boy made a signal. Two men dressed like farmers came out onto the porch of the farmhouse. They did not seem to be armed. After a brief conversation with the boy, the men motioned for me to come into the house and sit down. I tried to identify myself as an American. The boy soon disappeared with one of the men. I assumed that the man went to a partisan outpost or headquarters somewhere, while the boy went back to the cows.

The other man remained with me and made motions to ask me whether I was hungry. In this situation, sign language, pantomime, worked very well. It was late afternoon and approximately seven hours since breakfast. I had had nothing to eat since then and had run a couple of miles too. Of course, I nodded. "Yes."

The man cooked and served me a fried egg. Then he handed me a glass of rakija—a clear, poor brandy with a powerful kick. I ate. My host motioned for me to sit tight. So we waited, someplace south of my strafing run.

We tried to make conversation. The farmer tried pantomiming and gesturing and speaking a few words indicating that he had seen something of an air battle, or perhaps was describing my plane going through the sky on fire. I didn't think he could have seen much through the trees, but I was not going to argue. I hoped I was safe for the time being.

Judging by the hospitality I was being shown, I assumed that this man was a partisan, a name assigned to the factions of resistance to the Nazis. Given my location, he may have been one of the Yugoslav partisans, a resistance force under the command of Marshal Josip Broz Tito. It was around this time of Tito's leadership when the partisan resistance forces were being organized into the Yugoslav Army. None of this, obviously, came up in conversation.

Just around nightfall, a group of eight or ten men came into the farmhouse. They were unshaven and tough looking. These were indeed resistance fighters, members of the underground. Most were dressed in dark civilian clothes, but a few were in uniform. They all had guns of one kind or another.

I was introduced as a *"pilota Americana"* and shook hands with everyone. Names really meant nothing. They didn't want anybody but their close friends to know their names. Everybody was smiling and happy-ish, drinking rakija. I don't remember eating anything more, but I do remember drinking a lot of rakija. The partisans seemed to be having a party for having rescued me. We drank and then drank some more and tried to talk.

One of the fellows admired my .45 automatic and somehow made me understand that he wanted it. I hesitated. Finally I decided, first, that I would be unable to defend myself against such a large group anyway if they suddenly turned hostile. Second, these guys had been fighting the Germans on the ground, and I didn't want to go on a raid with them. Third, I hoped we wouldn't have to defend this farmhouse tonight against a German attack. I decided, finally, that the partisan could do more with the gun than I could, so he'd better have it in case he needed to defend either me or himself. I gave it to him with a smile. The fighters convinced me that I should stay there for the night and they would take care of me. Another drink of rakija, and I got very sleepy.

One may wonder how I could sleep that first night behind enemy lines. Wasn't I too anxious? The truth was that I was simply exhausted. The Yugoslavians had told me I was safe. I was forty-five miles from the Germans. I was with a bunch of partisan soldiers, patriotic to their country—enemies of my enemy. One of them had wanted my .45, and I had decided it was better for him to have it than for me to keep it. I could have woken up dead, but I felt pretty secure. Besides, when you're tired enough, you can sleep.

Early the next morning, I woke up with not even a hangover. I was informed that someone would carry me farther south. I looked outside, and here came this little old lady and a small, skinny man—husband and wife—with two of the tiniest horses you might ever see. Behind the horses was a very small flatbed wagon, which they indicated I should climb onto. It was equipped with a pile of hay to cushion the ride.

I got on, and off we went. The road was not too rough, only mildly hilly, and I rode sitting on the hay, lying on the hay, with my feet on the hay, or with my legs over the side—any way I could find comfort for a little while on a long and boring ride through the countryside. Long or even slightly steep hills were hard for those little horses, so whenever they pulled up, I got off and walked to lighten the load. The couple and I couldn't communicate much, but we understood the conditions. They were going to deliver me somewhere.

At this stage of the war, as I came to learn, the German occupation was primarily concerned with defense of the main roads and railroads within the country. They could move troops and supplies by guarding trains and convoys. Between these main thoroughfares, which ran all different directions, were areas the size of, say, a small county, in which the partisans could live relatively normal lives. If their resistance fighters went out to stop a courier on the main road or blew up the railroad tracks or something like that, the Germans would send a force to drive the partisans back into the woods. They might burn a few buildings in a small village or one of the little bridges over the local stream. They might even burn a couple of villages. Afterward, the German patrols would go back to their main roads, and normal life would resume. We, the partisans and I, were free to move about the countryside within our circumscribed boundaries.

As our wagon made its slow progress from village to village, I noted that half the buildings were war-damaged or completely bombed out. Other buildings that remained were quite livable. Villagers would come out of the doors to see us, to get a look at a Black American pilot. The driver would stop the wagon and explain things to the local Communist commissar and the people around him. These groups of people were only halfway curious. They were, after all, war victims. Some of the bombs that had fallen on these places had been dropped from American bombers earlier in the war. Nobody loved death from the sky or the men who delivered it, either friend or foe.

In every village, it seemed, there was a raggedy old man with a loud mouth and a lot of missing teeth, who would yell at me, "I been America!

You been Pittsburgh? You been Gary? God damn!" Or he might name some other big steel or factory town like Seattle or Birmingham. It was an apparent attempt to be friendly and to be recognized as a big shot. He was using all the English he could remember.

The truth was, yes, he had been to America! He may have run away from military duty in any one of the little European countries in existence there before World War I—nations such as Bosnia, Serbia, Croatia, Montenegro, and others that combined to form Yugoslavia and have since broken apart again. At any rate, in America, this guy likely worked in a steel mill, a manufacturing plant, or a mine. He could work anywhere in the country, because in America he could not be drafted to fight. He was not an American citizen. He might have earned high wartime wages, lived frugally, and saved his money. When the war ended, he returned home a rich man. He may have lived like a prince for twenty years or so until the money ran out. When World War II came along, he was too old for military duty, too old to work, too old and too poor to return to America. He was just eking out his last miserable days. I felt sorry for him until I remembered that these guys had worked in good jobs in America—jobs that were off limits to Blacks in those days.

Introductions were repeated several times during this one-day journey as we traveled from village to village. I began to feel that I was just an object on display to show how the partisans were helping America. Toward evening, when I was more than ready for the trip to end, we arrived in the large town of Glina, where the partisan headquarters was located. There had been no fighting here; Glina was completely intact.

At the partisan headquarters, I was questioned a little out of military necessity, but I was not grilled per se. I was given an identification pass and told I could sleep in a room on the second floor of a hotel building.

The hotel had a muddy courtyard with a well in the middle. There had been plenty of horses around, so I figured that the water was not drinkable unless it was purified. I had a rubber bladder and water purification pills in my escape kit, so I tried using them—once. Thereafter, I drank only wine or rakija. Taverns were open to the public, so obtaining something to drink was not a problem. Here in Glina, I also decided that I would never again complain about US Army food no matter how bad it seemed. The reason was simple; I had a chance to experience the partisan mess.

For the partisans, food preparation began with the noon meal. Potatoes were boiled with meat in a huge pot. Only the cooks knew what kind of meat they served. When your turn came to eat, you were given a spoon, a bowl with some of the stew—a piece of potato, maybe some meat—and a piece of bread. The bread was made from coarsely ground corn and a little fat of some kind and baked in a ball in a hearth oven. The outside was a hard, chewable crust; the inside, an inedible goo. For the evening meal, beans and water were added to the pot, and the noon meal was repeated. For breakfast the next day, the evening stew had been cooked down to gravy. A little gravy, a piece of bread, and a warm brown substitute for coffee served as that meal. If anything remained in the bowl after the first eater, more stew was added to it and the bowl was passed to the next person. Easy, no KP!

Sharing the room with me, without beds, were five young Frenchmen who had been prisoners of the Germans and then freed by the Russians. They were walking back to France wearing striped prisoner-of-war uniforms and little else, and they had six or seven hundred miles left to travel. The partisans would not feed them regularly or give them much help; the French were merely permitted to walk through their country. These guys did not look strong, but they appeared to be in remarkably good health considering the ordeal they must have gone through.

Dunkirk had occurred in 1940, when many French soldiers were left behind and captured by the Germans. It was now 1945. Only these men knew how long they had actually been prisoners. Some of them could speak a little English. They saw the American flag on my jacket and thought I might be able to help them somehow; they, too, never questioned my skin color. I did give them some money to buy a few potatoes and some tobacco from the farmers' market. I even bought some tobacco for myself. The Frenchmen showed me how to roll the leaves and shave off tobacco for a cigarette, but I have forgotten how I smoked it. We walked together around the town and got along all right. I was simply exploring, although there was nothing to see that I remember. These men were looking for anything they could find in the way of food and creature comforts.

While walking around Glina, I saw the partisan women soldiers for the first time. They wore heavy, woolen British uniforms, caps bearing red felt stars, and high-top shoes, not boots in the European style. They also wore woven military ammunition belts and suspenders. Two hand grenades were attached where the suspenders hooked on. The Germans had raped and pillaged their way through Yugoslavia, killing anybody and anything that they wanted. These women had trained as regular soldiers as a matter of survival and revenge. They had risked their lives on the front lines and in guerilla raids. When the partisan boss offered me an opportunity to be with one of them, I turned the offer down. He had the power to ask anything of them, and they would do it, but they were not prostitutes. They did not deserve to be treated as anything other than the professional fighters they were.

After a couple of days in Glina, I asked at partisan headquarters when I would be moved on. They were noncommittal. My French roommates mentioned hearing of a British mission in the next town, which was seven or eight miles away. I asked the partisans to take me there but received no commitment.

"When?" I asked.

Again, no commitment. I began to understand. I was of more value as a showpiece, a feather in their cap, rather than a military personage to be returned to duty with his own forces. Or maybe I meant nothing either way. I requested, and received, permission to walk to the next town.

The British-intelligence mission was in the town of Topusko (pronounced "TOE-pus-koh"). I was given a pass for travel identification by partisan headquarters. I had been with the partisans for five days and was anxious to get back to Italy. The next morning, the five Frenchmen and I set out walking to Topusko. We walked along at a leisurely pace in bright sunshine. The Frenchmen had been walking a long time and were not fast travelers anymore. I was the only one excited. This was to be a meeting of Allies! It turned out to be a great disappointment for the French. The British mission would do nothing for them. Why that was the case was never explained to me.

For me, Topusko turned out to be the best place to be at this time in the war. The mission was located in a substantial two-story wooden house with about ten rooms, including six bedrooms. It was staffed by Captain Richard Byrd and two sergeants. The sergeants were veterans from El Alamein and Tobruk who had chosen a different type of service to finish out the war, although this service had its dangers as well. The mission was also staffed with a cook and stocked with supplies provided by Allied parachute drops.

No other airmen were staying at the mission at the time I arrived. The captain questioned me briefly and soon phoned partisan headquarters—for what reason I didn't know. I did learn later that I had been accepted as an American airman at face value. After all, I couldn't possibly have been German, and Black airmen were not new to them. The captain had "rescued," for want of a better term, other Black fighter pilots—namely Shelby Westbrook, Robert Chandler, and Emile Clifton, all from the 99th Fighter Squadron. Clifton was a magician by profession. The captain identified him as a "conjurer"; I knew him as a classmate. The captain and I did not discuss my unit or our target, just bare details. After sizing me up, he went to a storeroom and returned with a bundle of clean clothes and a bar of soap for me.

The mission stocked clean uniforms, underwear, socks, blankets, and shoes. Any airman could lose boots when bailing out of an airplane if he hadn't laced them tightly. Bomber crews, especially, failed to do that while on eleven-hour missions. If they had to bail out of a plane, *wham*, their boots would fly off. Back on the ground, if they had no shoes, they would have to walk barefoot or in stocking feet until they arrived at a place such as this, where they might find some kind of foot protection. In fact, the mission had everything a downed Allied airman might need. Besides food and clothing, I found that there were toothpaste and toothbrushes; whiskey, either American or British; and American cigarettes and tobacco. Supplies aside, here was a safe, dry place to sleep, and now I could even take a bath. Topusko, it turned out, was a spa town with natural hot spring baths that dated back hundreds of years.

A partisan soldier had been sent to escort me to the bath. Maybe he could not believe I was an officer, because he took me to the enlisted men's bath. This was a large, circular concrete pool in a dingy, poorly lighted building. The stalls for washing were small and gray, but the privilege of soaking in a body of hot water was wonderful. It was now March 9. It had been months since I'd had a tub bath or shower and six days since I'd had a chance to wash up or remove my clothes at all. I scrubbed away the accumulated grime, then changed into the clean uniform and underwear I had been provided. I brought my own clothing, properly identified as mine, back to be laundered. Following a good dinner at the mission, I was shown a room where I could sleep. I was warm and clean and under clean blankets. Almost heaven.

The next day, I was sent to the local hospital. It appeared to be a converted multistoried school building. I explained to the doctor my ordeal with the parachute. He examined me with a stethoscope and began looking at my back, feeling for broken bones. When the exam ended, he ordered me to bed. This was a real surprise. I thought the doctor was showing off for Captain Byrd. In the hospital, nothing was too good for me. I even had some chicken-and-rice soup and an American cigarette.

The hospital was far away from any frontline battleground, and it was only half-filled with patients. Here were men recovering from serious wounds, many of them caused by exploding mines and shell fragments. I learned a few words of the Croatian language. I assumed the hospital was situated there so they could take advantage of the healing powers of the hot baths, but I didn't see any patients go to the baths. After two days and one night in this place, I decided that these seriously wounded men needed care; I did not. I signed myself out and returned to the mission.

The British-intelligence mission in Topusko was in one of the partisans' relatively safe areas. As the days went by, several other downed airmen came into the mission, singly and in pairs. I wondered how the captain could be confident that they were not Germans posing as Allied airmen. He took each name, rank, and serial number and radioed them back to Allied headquarters. I don't know what he found out about them or whether he really trusted them, but we all got along very well. Except in one instance, I can recall no discrimination.

Sometimes the partisans held dances, and the exception to my harmony with other guests occurred once when I got up to dance. I stood up, and someone stopped the music. I was not allowed to dance. This would not have come from the local population; it was the Americans who took measures to keep the races separate in Europe. I never learned who among the mission guests had a problem with my dancing, but since there didn't seem to be much I could do about it, I pushed the insult out of my mind. Maybe I should have remembered this incident during the return trip, but here, for the most part, we were like one big, happy family.

The routine in Topusko was better than at a rest camp. We awoke to hot tea and toast made with good bread (not the partisan bread) baked daily.

After washing up and brushing our teeth, we headed for the bath, but now we went to the officers' bath. This was a clean, brightly lit, tiled immersion pool, around which were individual tiled shower rooms for washing prior to entering the pool. This pool was so hot that one inched his body down into it, hanging on to the poolside ledge, descending one step at a time. Nobody went under! We would soak for about half an hour.

Some days, we stopped at a tavern on the way home for a glass of rakija. No one had much money, because not every man had received an escape kit. Shortages occurred, often after too many bombers failed to make it back from their missions. Their squadrons would not have enough kits available to cover every man on the next mission.

There were different escape kits for different situations; mine was a plastic box about 5"×7"×1". It contained a map printed on silk; maybe forty dollars in US currency; a rubber water bag; water purification pills; fish hooks and line; matches, I think; hard candy; and maybe first aid or pain pills. The forty dollars in American money made us rich. Just one dollar was worth ten times the local currency, and in most cases the local currency would become worthless after the war anyway. All Europeans wanted American dollars.

It was the custom that when guys from different Air Corps outfits met, they would exchange pieces of paper currency they had signed. We taped or glued our collections of signed American and foreign currencies together and folded them into our wallets. This was just a little souvenir of the war—evidence that we had met these people. We called the currencies we collected our "short-snorter bills," named after the pilots they represented. You see, even before federal regulations restricted pilots' use of alcohol, airmen discovered that it was not a good idea to drink heavily before flying. They learned to drink less than a full shot, or a "short snort," and so they became known as "short snorters." If you didn't have your short-snorter bill when drinking with another pilot, you had to buy drinks. If he didn't have his, he would buy drinks.

I found other ways to pass the time, too, while waiting to be returned to my unit. The mission had some magazines and a few books I could read in the afternoons. Sometimes I walked around the town and looked at the many closed bath buildings. Topusko, as I learned over time, had been inhabited since antiquity. Its hot springs were used to heat homes during the days of the Roman Empire.

Another structure that caught my eye was a ruined Gothic church. As I learned many years later, this symbol of Topusko's past was the chapel of the Blessed Virgin Mary of Pohod, built by King Andrew II of Hungary in 1233. The chapel stood until it was destroyed by Turkish troops in 1558.[31] Portions of the old walls in front of me were covered with vines. The area was like a park: all grass. No one was available to answer my questions about it, either because of the language barrier or because the people were uninterested. At that time, finding enough food to stay alive was more important to the locals than any landmark, and who could blame them?

One day I decided to go fishing. I cut a pole, dug some worms, and sat for a while on the riverbank. Someone came by—a partisan, I think—and indicated that I was wasting my time. When the partisans wanted fish, they dropped a grenade into the water and killed all aquatic life nearby. Then they could simply scoop all the floating fish into a boat. Now there were no fish.

Another afternoon, I invented the sport of frog-flipping. Using a flexible tree limb, I would slip one end under a swimming frog and, with a flick of the wrist, flip the frog out of the pond and several feet into the air, sometimes many feet from the water. Was this cruel? It passed a few hours.

I learned that the reason I could not get back to Italy yet was simple logistics. Because the Germans controlled the roads, it was unsafe to drive out. And now that it was spring, the ground had thawed enough that it was impossible to fly out. The field was too soggy for a C-47 cargo aircraft to land without the danger of getting bogged down.

A C-47 could, however, drop supplies by parachute on a day secretly scheduled by radio. At the appointed hour, the plane flew over the field, and the crew threw out their loads. The cargo parachutes opened, but not all the crates came down on the field. This was our excitement for that day. We watched the fall and chased the parachutes into the woods, then dragged the crates back to the field. All sorts of supplies were dropped: food, cigarettes, whiskey, clothes. There were no guns or ammo for the partisans. That was not part of this mission.

---

[31] Wikipedia, s.v., "Topusko," last modified June 11, 2023, https://en.wikipedia.org/wiki/Topusko.

CHAPTER 10

BACK TO RAMITELLI

While I was still at Topusko, the partisans completed reconstruction of a bridge over a major river in the area, the River Glina. They'd had a temporary bridge, but the newly repaired one made crossing the river much easier, and this called for a big celebration. About half the townspeople walked out to a huge meadow near the bridge. The bigwigs got up on a platform constructed for the occasion and made speeches.

A small biplane trainer was flown into the meadow for the celebration. Talk about a frail contraption! It was constructed of fabric and wire, but it did fly. After all the speechmaking, the pilot put on a nice little air show. He performed loops and turns and dives, which thrilled the crowd.

After the show, I was asked if I wanted to fly the plane. The answer in my mind was a great big capital "NO." Go up in that flimsy little thing and kill myself just to prove that I could fly an airplane? Uh-uh. If I should have to get killed, I wanted it to be in service to my country, not from showing off.

I very, very politely declined. I didn't even try to get close to that plane. The celebration finally ended, and we returned to the mission, my desire to get back to flying in the war stronger than ever.

One day, early in the afternoon, we were jolted by the flat, loud, continuous *bra-a-a-a-ack* made by a pair of Messerschmitt-109 fighter planes. The sound, which seemed to be coming from the north, was absolutely terrifying. I thought it was an air raid.

I peered out from the south side of the house. The planes went by without firing a shot, but their passing sent the partisan townspeople into a panic. They knew what an attack sounded like, and they were convinced that they were going to be attacked this time. They disconnected pumps at the bathhouses and threw them into wells. They manned their antiaircraft guns. Much of the population prepared to leave town.

Captain Byrd telephoned a friend upon whom he relied for intelligence. He reported to us, the US airmen at the mission, that there would be no attack. He was right, it seemed, and we almost relaxed. Then the noise came back. The planes were headed north this time. The antiaircraft batteries, now ready, opened up. They hit nothing—only air behind the planes—and the planes flew on. These Messerschmitts must have been equipped with noisemakers meant to deliberately frighten people on the ground. Our P-51s certainly were not that loud. If a person stood on the ground in the path of a P-51 and didn't see it, they would not know it was there until it had already passed by.

One day, Lieutenant Colonel Thaxton, a P-38 pilot, arrived at the mission. He was as happy as anyone else to have reached a place of safety. At one point early in our acquaintance, he commented on the bravery of the P-51 pilots to have flown so far with just one engine. I reminded him that he was here on the same ground and he had started with *two* engines. I refrained from mentioning the inferior Allison V-12 engines used in the P-38, and Colonel Thaxton never told me what had actually happened to bring him here. No one had to provide information to anyone except Captain Byrd, and we didn't. Personal stories were never exchanged.

On nights when the captain was to communicate by radio to his headquarters, he composed his material and encoded it for transmission by Morse code, not by voice, with the help of his sergeants. They would send this message back to wherever headquarters was located—I don't think it was England, perhaps someplace in Italy—and they were quite secretive about it. I was never invited to participate—and rightly so, I thought. But somehow Colonel Thaxton had established his credibility. Maybe he had secret words to pass on or something that I didn't have, because, to my surprise, only a couple of nights after he arrived, he was helping them encode the messages. I never found out how the captain knew he could trust him.

The colonel and I got along well. At some point, he borrowed my remaining thirty-two dollars in American money to buy a woman's embroidered costume. He wanted to give his wife a souvenir, but he, too, had flown without an escape kit. He paid me back later in Italy.

The greatest highlight of my stay in Yugoslavia was the invitation accorded me as an officer to watch a battle. Captain Byrd had a close friend, a necessity in this war situation, who was high in the partisan ranks. His name was Major Udelitz.

When the captain asked, courtesy of Major Udelitz, "Do any of you guys want to go watch a battle?" I jumped at the chance.

The next morning, about three o'clock, we tumbled out. Major Udelitz, his driver, Captain Byrd, Colonel Thaxton, and I left about four o'clock on a very cold morning. The five of us packed into a low staff car of German make. The driver handled it like a maniac road-race champion even though the roads were narrow and winding, with sharp curves. And, of course, they were in very bad condition. I don't know how many potholes were actually bomb holes. After traveling south for two or three hours, daylight arrived, but I couldn't tell where we were. This was as far as the driver was going. We got out, stretched, and had a cup of what was supposed to be coffee—the warm, brown substitute I had encountered before. Then Major Udelitz asked us whether we could ride horseback.

Couldn't "The Greatest Pilot in the World" do anything? Of course I must be a good horseback rider! Okay, I could get on a horse, and if it didn't try to throw me off, I could ride. Captain Byrd was, of course, an expert horseman because of his British military training, and he was anxious to exhibit his skill. Major Udelitz was a pretty good horseman too. Colonel Thaxton was game, although he had never ridden. The four of us mounted up after a little stirrup fitting, and we rode carefully for about twenty minutes as we got accustomed to riding.

Then the captain wanted to race. So we raced! Downhill, uphill, on the flat—it's extremely lucky that there was no jumping of fences or brooks or obstacles. Yes, I was scared! What a hell of a way to get killed—thrown from a horse in the middle of nowhere, Yugoslavia. After a while, maybe the horses got tired. Maybe the captain finally noticed the colonel and me. We had gone along with the program, but we were clearly hanging on for dear life. Whatever the reason, the race was finally called off. The captain had had a ball; the colonel and I had had an experience.

We rode for an hour before we finally reached a position somewhere near the rear of a battle area. Now we were invited to climb a steep hill to a field artillery position. The climb wasn't difficult, but we had to scramble on the loose stone. We climbed up and around with no specified trail to follow. Finally we reached the top, sore, tired, and hungry. We had arrived at a field artillery post in a rear echelon position, about two thousand feet above the valley floor and roughly five miles from Bihać, the town involved in the battle. That was *almost* far enough for me.

We could see a few spires sticking up within the village and a large smudge of dust, presumably where the fighting was the heaviest. We didn't really know what was happening. Major Udelitz explained the situation to Captain Byrd and Colonel Thaxton, but his description did not make a lot of sense to me. There were four or five men and an officer at the observation position, and they had a telephone line to men on the gun crew.

Whenever the gun crew got a phone call from the observation point, they would load and fire off a few rounds from their 75 mm gun, which was aimed at the town. I assumed their target was somewhere within the dark smudge, but I could not observe any hits. These guns did not make a big noise, only a resounding *whump* upon firing, followed by the *whirp-whirp* of a shell flying away. If any Germans had bothered to locate this gun source, they could have hit us. Their 88 mm guns were accurate. But no fire came our way. I looked at my map and located our approximate position, but I could not accurately figure out the German position. I knew they were between us and the Dalmatian Coast, located far south of the city.

After observing what I really couldn't see for over an hour, I sat down. It was nearly midafternoon. We had been up since three that morning and hadn't yet had anything to eat. I fell asleep right where I was sitting. Sometime later, I awoke to find that our group was being sent back down the mountain. We scrambled down and walked awhile, then rode trucks to a town called Slunj. The captain disappeared with some partisan officers. The colonel and I were invited into a nondescript building to await dinner.

Eventually, a partisan bigwig brought in a gallon-sized can with a green label. No one seemed to know for sure what was in it, because the label was printed in German.

He gave it to me and the colonel, who said, "What are we going to do with it?"

"I think it must be food," I said, "so maybe we've got dinner."

We managed to communicate to one of the women there that we wanted to have the can opened so we could see what was in it. They opened it.

"Martin, what's in there?"

"It looks like stew."

I made motions for the contents to be heated and served. It was stew, with meat and potatoes. The heated dish was brought out, and I became the official taster. Nothing ill came of that, so we ate as much as we wanted. It tasted all right. A bowl of stew along with a piece of bread made the meal—a good meal.

When we had finished, we were expected to take the can with us because it was still three-quarters full. The bigwig and the women retrieved the can for us, but the colonel and I both told them, "We don't want it. You keep it."

We had never heard so many thank-yous as we received from these cooks and helpers. The common people fighting with the partisan forces did not normally get to eat food intended for the officers and the high muckety-mucks. They were really thankful to get that stew.

Slunj, Croatia. Night had come. We were stranded but well fed, so we sat.

Finally, the captain returned and said, "I'm going with the partisans. There's going to be a truck to take you back to Topusko."

Sure enough, two high-railed, open-backed trucks loaded with civilians and soldiers eventually arrived. Both men and women were on board. The soldiers had guns. We did not. We climbed aboard, and off into the night we crawled.

The occupants of the truck were happy. They were celebrating. They cheered and sometimes burst into song. These partisans must have been at the battle. It seemed as though the Battle of Bihać had been won, although we couldn't know for sure. The soldiers had burp guns, and they were shooting them off—*bop-bop-bop-bop-bop!* Some guy would feel good, and *vroop!* he'd fire off some rounds.

The colonel and I crouched on the floor, thinking, *Who's gonna get killed?* We hoped the truck would not hit a bump that caused one of these guys to lose his balance and accidentally shoot fellow passengers.

We rode for about three-quarters of an hour, then the truck came to a halt. Everybody had to get out. *Okay, this is a rest stop,* we thought. Only it wasn't intended as such. Ours were refueling stops; the drivers had to recharge their fuel tanks. First, they got out and stirred up the fires in the generators. Then they foraged for wood to burn and distill in the generators. After about twenty minutes, when the accumulator tank showed enough pressure to start and run the engine for a while, everybody climbed back on, and we would chug into the night.

The trip took three or four hours. It seemed to go on forever. Each hour, we had to stop to create more gas so these trucks would run. It was almost morning when we finally reached Topusko, happy to be back.

The partisan fighters had indeed won the Battle of Bihać. This city, which had been claimed by various empires throughout history, was occupied by Axis troops during most of World War II. In 1941, a fascist group called the Ustaša murdered twelve thousand to fifteen thousand citizens—mostly Serbian, but also Jewish and Romani people—at an extermination location near Bihać. The partisans took control of the city in 1942, and for a brief time it was the center of Tito's partisan resistance. Then the Germans recaptured Bihać in 1943 and held control there until the battle I witnessed on March 28, 1945.[32]

The partisan victory opened the road out to the coast for us. Now I could get back to Italy! The Germans were forced to backtrack around the mountains in the area, exit to the north, and then head west back to Germany. We could ride out in trucks instead of walking out.

A few days after the Battle of Bihać, Captain Byrd announced our departure. By that time there were nine of us waiting to leave, including the colonel and me and personnel from various bomber units: a first lieutenant, two second lieutenants, and four sergeants.

I don't remember saying any good-byes—no handshakes, no embraces, not a single "Until we meet again." I must have said thanks somehow, though, because I certainly was grateful.

A couple of trucks arrived for us—good Ford trucks, high-walled and filled with shelled corn and beans. They were carrying food to the coast for

---

[32] Samuel Matthews, *Bosnia and Herzegovina: History, People, Culture, Travel and Tourism, Environment* (Global Print Digital, 2017), https://www.hoopladigital.com/play/14694219, 27.

the starving comrades in the newly liberated areas. We climbed in on top of the corn and beans and rode away. After about three hours, the trucks began climbing the landward side of the coastal range of mountains. They were not so bad, as mountains go.

Somewhere in the high middle plateau of the range, we passed above the famous Plitvice Lakes. This area would be established as a national park in 1949; in fact, it is the oldest and largest national park in modern-day Croatia. We looked down on a beautiful, peaceful mountain valley containing a few trees and a number of lakes and waterfalls. The water was an amazing light turquoise color, too pretty to be real because it was not the reflected color of the sky. I found out that the color of these lakes—sometimes sky blue, sometimes aquamarine, vivid green, or gray—varies according to their mineral content or the number of organisms living there.[33] I thought I saw more than one hotel there; in fact, the place looked like a resort. I made a mental note that if ever I decided to return to this part of the world, I would visit this place for sure. But I never got the urge to go back.

The remainder of the ride was mostly switchbacks down the steep coastal side of the mountains. The drivers took those turns very carefully. Even so, those of us riding in the back tried to help by moving to the inside of each turn. It was too late in the war for us to get killed by going over the side of a mountain. Toward evening, the trucks brought us directly to the American airfield at Zara, now known as Zadar. We climbed down, happy to be so much closer to home. It had taken a whole day to drive 120 miles as the crow flies. At Zara, we were given a meal and a place to sleep, possibly in a Quonset hut, before we could continue on the next leg of our journey.

The next day, we sat and waited for the plane that would fly us back to Italy. I found a discarded flare case and started carving in the soft aluminum, marking it with the dates of my eventful stay: 3/3–4/8, 1945, along with the names of Topusko and Zara, the beginning and end of this part of the trip, and Rakovica, a village near the Plitvice Lakes, just in case I ever wanted to return. The flare case would serve as a backup for the calendar I had created on the back of my map. Around midafternoon, we boarded a C-47 for the flight to Bari, Italy, the location of the Fifteenth Air Force Headquarters. We were quartered for the night in Bari.

---

33   Fodor's Travel, *Essential Croatia* (El Segundo, CA: Fodor's Travel Guides, 2021), 218, EPUB.

The following morning, I was escorted to a huge college building and taken to a small office on the second floor to be officially interrogated about my stay in Yugoslavia. Well into the interview, suddenly we heard air shrieking through the cracks around the doors and windows. The whole building began to shake, and glass came flying. I can't remember hearing a boom or an explosion.

I got up from my chair and moved into the arch of a closet doorway in case the ceiling collapsed. Looking down to the courtyard from the window, I saw soldiers and civilians running in all directions, and I heard screaming from people who were either frightened or hurt. Broken glass was everywhere. Large pieces of stone that had broken free from buildings made an obstacle course for the people running toward shelter. Signs with huge red arrows and the words "Al Ricovero" ("To Air Raid Shelter") were visible from my second-floor vantage point, but there was no way I could get there. Through it all, my interrogator sat calmly behind his desk.

When my interrogation was complete, we set out to discover what had happened. In the harbor, a mile or more away, a freighter loaded with ammunition had blown up. The blast blew out most of the windows in the city. I never heard how many people were killed or injured in that blast; officials didn't reveal much in the way of statistics.

After determining that it was safe to be out on the street, I walked around the town, looking for a place to eat lunch. Unfortunately, it seemed that all the restaurants in Bari were closed because their windows had been shattered. Not finding any place to eat, I headed back to the airfield for the last leg of my journey back to Ramitelli. I arrived to find, to my great surprise and delight, my old pal and classmate Frank Roberts. He was waiting there with a piggyback P-51D (a two-seater) to fly us home.

Frank Roberts and me.

You may have heard of evadees or escapees who have walked back from enemy territory at night, hidden in barns or even under haystacks or manure piles by day, gotten across rivers when they didn't know how to swim, and arrived back at a friendly base simply a bag of skin and bones. Not me! I was so fat I could hardly squeeze into the backseat of the plane. The flight to Ramitelli was delightfully uneventful. By April 10, I was safe at home.

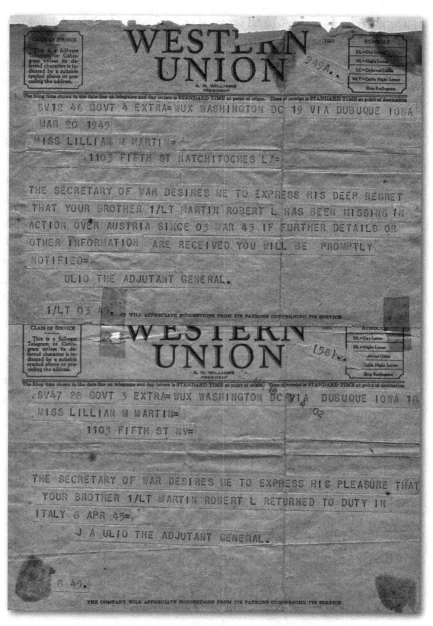

*Telegrams informing my family of when I was missing
in action and when I returned to duty.*

It was very damned good to be home again at Ramitelli. Of course the guys at the base greeted me, but they had already been told that I was safe, so it was no great surprise when I stepped out of the P-51 with Frank. I told my story to the intelligence officer of the squadron. Others before me had been shot down and returned, so I was no great curiosity. People were happy to see me, but they were busy. Our unit was preparing for a move farther north to Cattolica, Italy, 349 km up the Italian coast. We would be leaving Ramitelli.

When I returned, I discovered that the 332nd had gone even farther than before while I was on the ground in Yugoslavia. They had flown fighter cover to Berlin, Germany, a distance of eight hundred miles, on March 24. The P-51s had been outfitted with special fuel tanks to cover the distance. Getting the fuel tanks needed in time for the trip and figuring out how to attach them properly took a lot of ingenuity. This is a story of its own known as the Great Train Robbery. Once outfitted and on their way, three of our pilots each shot down one of Hitler's new Messerschmitt-262 fighter jets in spite of their far superior speed and firepower. Our entire group earned the Presidential Unit Citation for that trip. I was not there or even with my squadron on that date, so I did not get that medal.

I had expected to continue to serve my country after returning to my unit, but I, along with all eight men who had been on the ground with me in Yugoslavia, were told we would be sent home. By April 30, I had orders in my hands.

"Outin Getin."

I saw the new field at Cattolica on Saturday, May 2, but by May 8, I was in Naples, where a ship waited to take me back to the USA.

Victory in Europe had been declared that day. As you can imagine, a lot of people were celebrating. That night, we were confined to quarters at the repo depot (pronounced "repel-deppel"), the replacement depot in Naples. No one was quite certain how the Italians would respond to the Allied victory, so we were not allowed to go into the city. We had gotten this far. The war was now over. There was no sense in getting killed at this point.

The next day, May 9, we were loaded onto our ship. Most of us bunked in the same cabin—below deck, just as on the trip over. The colonel had other accommodations. The ship left the harbor that night, bound for the States. We came back on a vessel that was lit at night! A number of nurses were returning home on the same ship, and people were up on deck, dancing and celebrating. Everybody seemed to have a good time.

Our little group, all of us who had sheltered at the British mission in Yugoslavia except the colonel, stayed together all across the Atlantic. Our ship arrived back in the USA at Newport News on May 20, 1945, and our group disembarked together. We went to the mess hall and ate together, and we came back and slept together in our cots and tents that night. The next day, we got on a train together and were on our way to Jefferson Barracks, just outside St. Louis. I was the only Black serviceman in the group, and we all got along quite well. You could even say we were chums.

Then we got off the train at Jefferson Barracks. It was late in the evening, around 9:00 p.m., when the other guys piled into a cab. I was told by the driver not to get in, and all my "friends" drove off without me. Our camaraderie was at an end. I was on my own. Welcome to the USA!

My memory of the next few hours is a little hazy. I found a Black taxi driver who was willing to take me. I gave him money, and he bought me a bottle of whiskey. I don't remember whether I boarded another train that night or stayed at a hotel.

By May 27 I was reunited with my family. I knew they had been informed when I went missing and again when I returned safely, but I don't imagine that they breathed freely again until I walked through my father's front door. Of course everyone wanted to hear about all my adventures, how I had been shot down, how I had jumped out of a burning fighter plane, what I did on the ground behind enemy lines, how I had survived. The war was over in Europe, and I was home! We talked and celebrated late into the night.

The next day, who should arrive but my shirttail cousin Henry Valentine—in a casket. He was not a true blood relative, but he was the son of my first stepmother's sister, and we were very close. As kids, we rode our bicycles together. Henry had been in training at Tuskegee to become a gunner in a bomber when he was killed in an airplane accident. I had gone across the ocean, had adventures and near misses and arrived home safely, and this kid never made it out of Alabama. It was terribly sad. I came home to a celebration and found myself mourning the loss of a close friend.

After a week or two at home, I was ordered to report to an army air force camp in California. Actually, they ordered me first to Atlantic City because that's where they were sending the Black servicemen. Signage I had seen clearly said that everybody living east of the Mississippi River would report to Atlantic City and anybody living west of the Mississippi would go to Los Angeles. I challenged the order sending me to Atlantic City because, of course, Dubuque is not east of the Mississippi. Finally they relented. I had won my case. I was sent to Fort MacArthur, California, just south and west of Los Angeles.

When I arrived at the camp, I learned that I would stay in Santa Barbara, at one of the hotels right on the beach. This was special treatment for people who had had it rough during the war—servicemen who had evaded or been captured by the Germans. I stayed there for about a week. During this time, I had a couple of days to relax and do nothing. Then a medical team checked my teeth and my general health. Those in charge wanted to see what condition I was in, to see whether they had a body they could ship somewhere else.

Afterward, somebody called me in, talked to me, and asked where I wanted to serve now. I told them I wanted to go to the South Pacific. After all, that's where the war was still going on. They said, "You're crazy; you're not going to the South Pacific." There was no place for Black fighter pilots in the Pacific theater. So why did they even ask?

All the returning Black pilots were sent back to Tuskegee. I went there too, but I didn't stay long. They wanted to make me an instructor in B-25s. I did that for a few weeks. The place was piling up with returning pilots not qualified to teach a bomber group, because we were not twin-engine pilots, and technical officers with no place in a bomber group. There really wasn't room for all of us who ended up there.

In August, the atomic bomb was dropped, and the war ended in the Pacific theater as well. Two or three weeks later, we were told that everyone with the necessary points could seek a discharge.

The line duly formed, and when it was my turn I said, "I have eighty-five points, and I only need fifty-eight, so look it up and see if I can't get out of here."

We were not free to leave until our orders came. There were points awarded for missions flown, points for the campaign ribbon that we had, and points for just going overseas. So my points added up, and they said I could go.

I had to wait for my final paycheck until I got to Sioux City Air Force Base. This was not a normal payday; it was when they figured out what we owed and what we did not owe. We had been issued certain equipment that was the property of the army. No matter which field we went to, if we stayed any length of time, we received certain things to use, and when we left, anything that belonged to the field had to stay there. I had a canteen and a mess kit; these had to be checked off. We were allowed to keep a certain number of pairs of pants, shoes, socks, and jackets, as well as an overcoat if it was winter.

Anything else that was issued still belonged to the army. They checked to see whether we were credited with the pay we were supposed to get and whether we owed for anything. Rations were valued at thirty-seven cents per day. This amount was due Uncle Sam out of our salary. We had to go around to the various offices to turn in any equipment that had been issued to us, or we had to swear that we did not have any of their equipment. Only after we had obtained all required signatures was it okay for us to leave the base. I was formally discharged from the army on November 20, 1945. Afterward, I continued to serve in the US Army Air Corps Reserves and earned the rank of captain.

Besides the Distinguished Flying Cross, while still in the service I was awarded the Purple Heart and the Air Medal with six Oak Leaf Clusters. In 2007 I received the Congressional Gold Medal at a ceremony at the Capitol Building in Washington, DC, that honored all Tuskegee Airmen, including support personnel.

Congressional Gold Medal ceremony.

In 2006, I was inducted into the Iowa Aviation Hall of Fame for service as a Tuskegee Airman. On June 10, 2013, recognition of my service was entered into the US Congressional Record.

In 2010, Simpson College honored all twelve Tuskegee Airmen from Iowa with the George Washington Carver Medal in recognition of our "inspiration to others, demonstrated leadership and conviction, and dedicated service to addressing humanitarian issues."

Carver, the noted botanist and inventor, had studied piano and art at Simpson College before he obtained his bachelor's and master's degrees at Iowa State and went on to teach and conduct research at Tuskegee Institute. Simpson College had admitted him after a university in Kansas had denied him entrance.

The reverse side of the medal I received bears Carver's quote, both simple and profound: "I discovered I was a man."

EPILOGUE

THE FIGHT CONTINUES

I arrived home with $52.20 in my pocket and decided to pay my alma mater a visit. Should my funds go toward more college education? After all, three years had passed since my graduation from Iowa State, and I was a little rusty in my engineering subjects. Would more coursework help me get an engineering job? I did not have to wait long for an answer. "No," the university said. My degree should be good enough.

Still, I was getting no engineering job offers, and by now I had a stack of rejection letters a couple of inches thick. If I wasn't going back to college, I had to get a job doing something. You can hold your head up high, but you have to eat. I went to Chicago, where my brother Hank lived. Then I tried Detroit. After all, I had been stationed there almost two months. I thought maybe I could get a job in the auto industry. Nothing seemed workable. I tried driving a cab. Then I worked for International Harvester in their tractor works heat treatment department, unloading tractor shoes from the furnace.

Chicago, 1946.

I kept hoping and believing that something better would come along, and finally it did, in the form of civil service exams. I passed the exams for the Chicago Park District. They had no engineering positions, however, so I became a junior draftsman for the CPD in 1947. The civil service exams were for different grades: junior, electrical, and senior draftsman. I went through all three levels of draftsman for the park district.

Three years after I had started working for the park district, I took exams for the city of Chicago, which had its own exam system. There we were told, at first, that war veterans got an additional five points added to their score. But after the grades were computed, we were told that military service would not earn bonus points. I talked to other guys, and we wrote a letter protesting the change as obviously unfair. Officials responded by saying, essentially, that they were running the civil service and that if we sued or insisted, they would cancel the exams. We backed down. I did well enough anyway to score high on the list.

There was a scale of positions on the engineering side and another on the union side. The union tried to say that I got no credit for my experience, which meant that I would not pass the exam. I wrote out the table of organization and showed that the two sides were doing essentially the same type of work and that exam titles were equivalent. Seeing this, the union accepted my argument and gave me the credit I deserved. They let me pass.

The union had control over civil service positions. Unions were as opposed to Blacks as anyone else, but once you had a union job, you could propose your relatives for apprenticeships they would not be able to get otherwise. This helped open the unions to Black workers. I was first at that time. There were a few other Black workers in the union, but they weren't working as engineers. We cracked the shell. I went to work for the city of Chicago in January of 1950.

At long last, I felt that I could marry and settle down to start a family, and I knew just the person with whom I wanted to settle down. I had met the beautiful Odette Ewell at a dance the previous fall, where it became evident that she loved music and dance as much as I did. She also happened to be both creative and brilliant.

Odette and I were married on August 27, 1950. This also happened to be the day she graduated with a master's degree in English from the University of Chicago. I'm forever grateful that she chose to attend her wedding that day instead of her graduation!

Odette and I sang and danced together. We traveled and skied. I also played tennis. But more than anything, I wanted children. I wanted a big, happy family such as my father had, yet, as Odette and I approached our third anniversary, we still had no children. That's when my doctor told me that if I wanted to have a family, I'd better stop playing tennis. Tennis was a whole lot of work, a strain on my system, and evidently my sperm count was too low or too tired to produce children. I promptly traded tennis for golf, and the children arrived—four of them in five years.

I had so much fun with my son and daughters! We all swam, skied, and traveled together, but we also worked hard to achieve what we did. As my father taught me, I taught my children the importance of a good education. This ethic passed to the next generation too. One of my two grandchildren competed as a mental athlete, which won him a trip to Europe with his mother.

Academic excellence was not limited to the children. Odette received a Ford Foundation Grant for PhD studies in 1969. She worked toward her PhD while teaching at the City Colleges of Chicago and finally received her doctorate in education from the University of Chicago in 1980. Odette continued to teach at the City Colleges until her health forced her to retire in 1990 after about twenty years of service.

I worked for the city of Chicago as an electrical engineer from January of 1950 until I retired in 1987, having given thirty-seven years of service. I designed street lighting systems for the city. Among other things, I supervised the lighting project on Lake Shore Drive when the S curve was straightened out.

The union required anyone working for the city to be a union member. I passed the exam but was not allowed to participate as a member. In fact, my family was threatened if I tried to join or if I went to any union meetings. Yet I was a union member. I paid union dues. Eventually, I received a plaque for fifty years of membership—without ever having attended a meeting!

The union counts a person's military service time toward seniority, but they did not want to allow mine to count. I was not given credit for my military service until after I hired a lawyer. My brother-in-law, Ray Ewell, a criminal attorney and a former state representative, won for me the military credit I was due. Small wonder in light of my challenges, I suppose, that two of my daughters became lawyers. One of them prosecuted employment discrimination cases for the Equal Employment Opportunity Commission and headed the National Council of EEOC Locals for twenty-two years.

One time I was up for a promotion in which I would supervise half a dozen people. I had passed the examination, but before I was offered the position, my records were examined, including my college grades and even my grades from high school. Everything I had ever done, it seemed, was scrutinized. And there were questions.

Had I been nominated for a superior public service award? No.

Had I participated in a management career development program? Yes, somebody had brought me along a little bit.

I really don't think other people faced the same level of scrutiny when they were promoted to higher positions.

Once my promotion was finally approved, there was the issue of compensation. In a normal promotion, one got a 5 percent increase in pay. I was running a particular section known as Electrical Project Design. My section was the one doing the projects that brought the big money into the department, yet my salary was not in line with the salaries of the people running all the other sections. I was supposed to get a new title with this position, but I said, "I can't take this promotion without a ten-percent increase in pay."

My immediate supervisor, a man of color himself, said he would back me for the position but he would not back me for the pay raise.

He said, "I can't give it to you. People will claim it's worse than nepotism if I promote you and give you a ten-percent raise."

He had just attained the title, "Deputy Commissioner of Bureau of Electricity." As a Black man just getting his own position, he knew he would not be allowed to promote every Black worker in his department. The white workers wanted promotions too.

I decided to talk to the head of the department. I made an appointment to see him, but the appointment I was given was after hours. I had to wait. While I waited, though, I wrote down people's salaries to prove that if I took this job at the rate they wanted to pay me, I would have people working under me with salaries higher than mine.

"It won't work," I told him. "I can't take the position."

He said, "I see your problem. You get the ten percent."

It's so easy to pass over a matter and say, "Well, that's just the way it is." But if you don't fight for these things, you don't get them.

In 1987, I was set to become the electrical design engineer, one step from the top. The Department of Streets and Sanitation had jurisdiction over the division of streetlights, and I would have been in charge of the streetlight division. But this was during the tumultuous years of Mayor Washington's tenure. The mayor went on a trip to San Francisco, and his opponents took the opportunity of his absence to install a man of Hispanic descent in the position I was supposed to have. I was expected to train their guy for my job.

Was it worth fighting this battle so late in my career? I had wanted to be a quiet support for the Black cause; I did not want to be in the limelight. I don't even like the term "Black America." What does that mean, anyway? I only want to be remembered as a good citizen. I decided to let this battle go. I retired.

I didn't even know until then that I had been an independent contractor all along and could have been fired at any time. But they knew they needed me. After I retired, they had to keep calling me back as a consultant.

The majority of my coworkers were Irish. Every day I would go to work and find on my desk jokes about Black people. Every day, it seemed, there was a running battle of Irish versus Black. I would bring the jokes home to my family in the evening, but I turned them around on the Irish. Finally, Odette told me I could not bring those things to dinner anymore. Over time, I earned the respect of my coworkers, and at least some of the hostilities ceased.

After the children were on their own, Odette and I continued to enjoy our joint and separate pursuits. I continued to play golf, having discovered that I really liked the sport. I played every chance I got, and by the time Odette and I flew to Hawaii long after the war—both to visit a tropical island and to see the damage at Pearl Harbor—I realized that Hawaii was the twenty-fourth state I'd golfed in. I decided then to set myself a goal to golf in every state in the union.

I've done that. I have played on one golf course, at least, in every state. Yes, I did find a golf course in Alaska, in Anchorage. I also played in Canada, Mexico, and Puerto Rico, and I played on a nine-hole course in the District of Columbia. I wish I'd been a good golfer. Being a hacker, I tried to play good golf.

The annual conferences of the Tuskegee Airmen, hosted in different places around the country, provided a vehicle for my golfing quest. One year we had a conference in Boston, so I rented a car there and drove west to New York and played outside of Albany. I had to get back to Boston because that's where I would catch my return flight, so, coming back, I played in Connecticut, New Hampshire, Maine, Rhode Island, and Massachusetts. That was six states in one trip! It cost about two hundred dollars each time, and yes, it was fun.

Every place I went, I told them the story about trying to play in all fifty states. I had played at Pebble Beach before that and in Los Angeles before Pebble Beach. We had a convention in Seattle, so I played there. We had one in Detroit, and I played in Detroit, and I then drove over the border to Canada and played there too. The air force has golf courses because big bases need a lot of athletic options for the soldiers. I played a course on a military base in Alaska. I also played on military bases in Washington, Alabama, and Mississippi, but mostly I played on civilian courses. I found only two Black-owned golf courses to play on. One was in New Jersey, the other in Ohio.

As soon as the snow started flying, early in November, ordinarily we gave up on golf for the season. But one year there was a notice in the *Chicago Tribune* about an "Eskimo Open" on Cog Hill. It said that the golf course would be open for play on the first Sunday in January the following year, and I decided to take the challenge. I woke up on the appointed day, ready to play golf, and found that it was ten degrees at Cog Hill. I put on long underwear and an extra pair of pants. I used rain gear because I didn't want to be weighed down with an overcoat, but I wore two or three layers of clothing; overshoes, not golfing shoes; and some warm gloves.

I had made my own gloves—mittens, really—out of denim cloth from an old pair of overalls, foam rubber, and insulated cotton cloth. Of course, there are ready-made gloves for anything you want to do in cold weather, but I couldn't find anything warm enough for this purpose, so I made my own. This was just to keep my hands warm between shots. I would pull my bag or take the cart, and when I got to my ball, I would take the mittens off, golf clubs at the ready, and hit the ball. There wasn't much wasted time this way. When I was not hitting the ball, these mittens allowed me to flex my fingers and hold on to the cart or pick up my bag of clubs.

One can get very practical when one needs to be. I was sewing buttons onto my clothing when I was four years old. I also pumped the treadle of my aunt's sewing machine on Saturday afternoons so that she could repair clothing, which of course everybody did in those days. Sometimes she made new clothes. With this background, it's probably no surprise that I invented a few things myself.

The Chicago chapter of the Tuskegee Airmen is named the DODO Chapter. I was an early member when it formed in the 1950s. As a speaker and educator for the Young Eagles program within the local chapter, I, along with others, visited schools to tell the story of the Tuskegee Airmen. We brought along photo displays. We talked to students and invited them to come out and take a free ride in an airplane. Every second Saturday, as weather permitted, we took kids flying for free as part of the Young Eagles flight program. This would allow them to see whether they might have an interest in aviation. In addition, the chapter encourages minority youth to pursue higher education and offers scholarships to students who fit certain criteria.

Needless to say, all this requires funding. Every year, the DODO Chapter holds a big fundraising event, its Mardi Gras Ball. We put on a show and serve New Orleans-style food for dinner. Through the years, various celebrities have come to headline the event. In 1991, for example, Miss America, Marjorie Judith Vincent, came and signed photos as part of a "Made in the USA" promotion.

Odette and me at one of the DODO Chapter's gala events.

For years I was very much occupied with helping to make our fundraiser a success. We had dancers for the event, and I was one of them. We worked each year with a professional dancer to create a new routine, and then we practiced that routine every week. It took a lot of commitment to get our moves down just right. Every winter found me so busy rehearsing the latest dance routine for our fundraiser that even invitations to play golf with friends in Florida did not tempt me.

Costumes were a part of the show, and of course I made my own. One costume I made was that of a clown with an invisible dog on a leash. One was a raisin, made from a black plastic garbage bag with glasses glued on. Once I was Count Dracula. My best creation, though, was when I bought a ten-dollar wedding dress and a tuxedo from the Salvation Army, pieced the tux out into a tail, and then sewed half of each into a single half-groom, half-bride costume. People were wowed.

My "half and half" costume.

I threw myself into whatever project I decided to take on. Our home in South Chicago was one hundred years old. Of course it needed some repair, but I also tried to restore it to its original glory. I built a workshop in the basement, complete with water access and walls, and then I set about to make other improvements. The old house had multiple fireplaces, but they were not functional. First I got them working properly as wood-burning fireplaces; later I converted them to gas and then electric to accommodate family allergies. When I decided that the house needed more ventilation, I installed—what else?—an airplane propeller on the roof. I was not trained as a carpenter, but I finished whatever work I did to the best of my ability. We turned that beautiful old high-ceilinged house into a gem.

After Central Alternative High School in Dubuque wrote a book on the Tuskegee Airmen in 1997, I became pen pals with the students and spent quite a bit of time corresponding with them. The administration, with the students' encouragement, eventually got corporate sponsors to fly me in, put me up in a hotel room, and drive me to the school. They sponsored a dinner and a symposium. It was all a bit overwhelming. People were lined up around the block, and they all, it seemed, had stories: "My grandfather ski-jumped with you. I didn't believe it …" They came with everything. "Would you sign this picture?" We could barely get in to start the program. It was so successful that they decided to do it again at Lourdes College in Dubuque.

In addition to the other honors I've mentioned, I received an award from the State of Illinois on September 8, 2007. I didn't go to Springfield to get it because I was not originally from Illinois, but a buddy brought it back to me. I was also awarded an honorary doctorate in public service from Tuskegee University. I joked that this made me a second-class doctor and that, since my wife also held a PhD, we had two doctors in the house. I could have received a French medal, too, if I had filled out the paperwork. I would have been called to the office of the ambassador, and he would have pinned it on my chest. We did get a lot of official recognition. Civilian appreciation in general came more slowly, if at all. Once, while I was in formal military dress, a woman asked me to carry her bags.

Flying for my country was the greatest adventure of my life. Even after the war was over, however, there were still plenty of battles to fight here at home. I have tried to choose wisely. I have endured my share of insult and hardship because of the color of my skin. I've stuck up for myself when I needed to. And I did everything I could to protect and prepare my family. In the end, I like to think that my contributions, both abroad and at home, did make a difference. I like to think that my sacrifices helped pave the way for generations of Black Americans after me.

For a time, I was president of our neighborhood association. I knew when neighbors were sick, and I did what I could to help. I fought for decent housing, paved alleys, neighborhood playgrounds with programs and equipment, and access to swimming pools. I fought for a neighborhood school and against predatory lending. I never joined the Masons, as my father did, but I have always been civic minded. From within the DODO Chapter, I also helped to get a portion of Interstate 57 in the Chicago area named for the Tuskegee Airmen.

Throughout the various positions I have held within the DODO Chapter and neighborhood organizations, as well as at work, I have insisted that rules mean something; they must be followed. I have always been steadfast in doing things right. This, too, is a legacy I leave to my children.

Through it all, I have maintained an avid interest in the world around me, even in my later years. I have earned certificates in computer programming. I read books and magazines, especially those on military aviation history and *National Geographic* and *Smithsonian*. I also read engineering journals, and I have begun to try my hand at writing poetry.

Maybe my retelling of the Tuskegee Airmen's story, as I did for many years, has inspired young people to rise above their own circumstances to be the best they can be. I hope that this account of my adventures will not only entertain but will also shed a little light on a different time. Maybe even the joy I have found in life in spite of all the hardship has helped to make this world a better place.

In 2017, I had the opportunity to meet Julia Erdely. She was only fifteen years old in 1944 when she and her family were taken from their home in Transylvania and imprisoned at Auschwitz. Neither her mother nor her father survived, but she, her two sisters, and her brother lived to see the liberation of the concentration camps. When she learned through a neighbor that a Tuskegee Airman lived nearby, she was determined to meet me and thank me for my part in her rescue. Sure, our assignment had been to protect bomber crews, but our influence turns out to have spread far beyond that. I don't believe I had previously met anyone for whom the war made such a personal difference. Allied involvement when it mattered meant life itself to Julia and generations after her. I guess my own gratitude to a Union Army Civil War veteran had come full circle.

Julia and me.

AFTERWORD

Bob "Fox" Martin left this earth for good on July 26, 2018. He lived to see the dedication, on September 18, 2016, of a new Tuskegee Wing at the Aquatorium in Gary, Indiana. The ceremony included the unveiling of a P-51 replica named in his honor.

Robert Martin spent the last ten years of his life in the Chicago suburb of Olympia Fields. It was fitting that a ceremony at the village hall in November 2019 recognized the naming of the Olympia Fields Post Office after him.

The main terminal building at Dubuque Regional Airport was named after Captain Martin in a ceremony to honor its native son on July 19, 2022. The crowd in attendance included local residents as well as family members and friends from across the country and across the pond.

To One Who Went That Way

I miss you
When you are away
On lonely nights
And beautiful days.

Your smile's not here,
Your laughter is gone,
A memory floating
To be found in a song.

I'll come to see you
Tho the path be long.
Things must be forgiven
As rights, never as wrongs.

I feel you miss me,
But you never say why.
I know you love me
'Cause you never said good-bye.

—Robert L. Martin, September 2012

BIBLIOGRAPHY

Bucholtz, Chris. *332nd Fighter Group: Tuskegee Airmen*. Long Island City, New York: Osprey Publishing, 2007.

Centers for Disease Control and Prevention. "The Syphilis Study at Tuskegee Timeline." *The US Public Health Service Syphilis Study at Tuskegee*. December 5, 2022. https://www.cdc.gov/tuskegee/timeline.htm.

Central Alternative High School Project. *Clarity of Hindsight*. Dubuque, IA. 1997.

Davis, Benjamin O., Jr. *Benjamin O. Davis, Jr., American, An Autobiography*. New York: Plume, 1992.

Fodor's Travel. "Zagreb and Inland Croatia." *Essential Croatia*. https://www.hoopladigital.com/play/14212970.

Francis, Charles E. *Tuskegee Airmen: The Men Who Changed a Nation*. Boston: Brandon Books, 2008.

Fruehling, Tom. "Lessons in Independence." The *Gazette*. July 2, 2000.

Graff, Cory. "How the Curtiss P-40 Got That Wicked Shark Grin." *Smithsonian Air & Space Magazine*. April 2020. https://www.smithsonianmag.com/air-space-magazine/when-shark-bites-180974484/.

Hardesty, Von. *Black Wings: Courageous Stories of African Americans in Aviation and Space History*. New York: HarperCollins, 2008.

Losey, Stephen. "Meet the First 'Top Guns.'" Military Officers Association of America. May 23, 2022. https://www.moaa.org/content/publications-and-media/news-articles/2022-news-articles/meet-the-first-top-guns/.

Martin, Robert. Letter to college classmate Verne Hudek, May 18, 1944. *African American Heritage Foundation of Iowa*, Cedar Rapids.

Matthews, Samuel. *Bosnia and Herzegovina: History, People, Culture, Travel and Tourism, Environment.* Global Print Digital. 2017. https://www. hoopladigital.com/play/14694219.

"Memorandum for the Chief of Staff: Employment of Negro Manpower in War." FDR Presidential Library and Museum. November 10, 1925. https://www.fdrlibrary.org/documents/356632/390886/tusk_doc_ a.pdf/4693156a-8844-4361-ae17-03407e7a3dee.

National Historical Society. *U.S. National Park Service Oral History Project.*

Peterson, Cassie. "The History of the Civilian Pilot Training Program: Preparing Future WW2 Pilots on a Massive Scale." *Plane and Pilot Magazine.* June 3, 2022. https://www.planeandpilotmag.com/news/ pilot-talk/the-history-of-the-civilian-pilot-training-program/.

Pratt, Sara E. "Benchmarks: March 17, 1944: The Most Recent Eruption of Mount Vesuvius." *Earth: The Science Behind the Headlines.* March 15, 2016. https://www.earthmagazine.org/article/ benchmarks-march-17-1944-most-recent-eruption-mount-vesuvius.

Rose, Robert A., *Lonely Eagles: The Story of America's Black Air Force in World War II.* Los Angeles: Tuskegee Airmen Inc., 1996.

Schwieder, Dorothy. "The Life and Legacy of Jack Trice." *The Annals of Iowa* 69, no. 4. Fall 2010. https://history.iowa.gov/history/education/educator-resources/primary-source-sets/iowa-leader-civil-rights-and-equality/ life.

Scott, Lawrence P. and William M. Womack, Sr. *Double V: The Civil Rights Struggle of the Tuskegee Airmen.* East Lansing: Michigan State University Press, 1998.

GLOSSARY

ack-ack	Antiaircraft fire
AGCT	Army General Classification Test
altimeter	The instrument in a plane used to measure altitude
angels	Altitude in thousands of feet
AO	Army officer
AT	Advanced trainer
beacon	A visual navigational aid on the ground that rotates or flashes to indicate the location of an airport, landmark, airway or obstruction
biplane	An airplane with two main wings stacked one above the other
bogie	Enemy aircraft
cadets	Military pilots in training
P/C	Preflight cadets
B/C	Basic cadets
A/C	Advanced cadets
cowl flaps	Small doors in the bottom of the engine cowling that can be opened and closed by the pilot to regulate cooling of the cylinders when the plane is taking off and climbing
deadstick landing	A type of forced landing when a plane has lost all power

debriefing	Reporting of a mission's actual events
EM	Enlisted men
ETA	Estimated time of arrival
firewall	Go full throttle
gpm	Gallons per minute
ground loop	Rotation of the plane on the ground
hp	Horsepower
hood	A training device that is worn on the head to restrict the view from anything outside the plane so that the pilot can only see the instruments, as would happen when flying in poor visibility
inline engine	An engine that has all its cylinders in a line
instrument	Flying instruction relying solely on the instruments in the aircraft, not what can be seen outside the plane
IP	Initial point; the point at which a bomber begins its bombing run
KP	Kitchen patrol; work in the kitchen
landing stages	The five phases of a normal landing: base leg, final approach, round out, touchdown, after-landing roll
link trainer	A simulated cockpit that allows a pilot to practice maneuvers without the danger of getting hurt
manifold	A system of pipes within the engine that carries the air and fuel mixture from the carburetor to each engine cylinder
MP	Military police
mph	Miles per hour
mess	Eating facilities
monoplane	An airplane with one pair of wings
moxie	Slang: courage, determination
OCS	Army officer candidate school

outside loop	A maneuver in which an airplane dives into a loop, is inverted at the bottom, then climbs back out of the loop and returns to normal straight and level flight
overcast	Clouds obscuring the sky overhead
pour the coal	Slang: speed up
PX	Post exchange—a store on a military base that sells food, clothing, and other items
Quonset hut	A lightweight prefabricated semicylindrical structure
radial engine	An engine in which cylinders radiate outward from a central crankcase like the spokes of a wheel
rakija	A clear, poor brandy
rpm	Revolutions per minute
rudder	A device located on the back edge of the airplane's vertical stabilizer, or fin, that can be moved to control rotation, or "yaw," of the airplane
sack time	Head back to the home field
shavetail	Derogatory term for a second lieutenant or newly commissioned officer
sideslipping	Moving the aircraft sideways while keeping the nose of the plane pointed in the same direction as before—a useful maneuver when landing in a crosswind
slide the movement	Slang: avoid going on missions
snap roll	A horizontal spin in the air
split S	A maneuver in which the pilot inverts the plane and descends into a half-loop, coming out upright and flying in the opposite direction at a lower altitude
stick	A device usually located on the floor of the cockpit that controls the airplane's attitude and altitude
three-point dead	Landing a plane on all three wheels at once and stopping immediately

throttle	A lever that controls the amount of fuel provided to the engine
undercast	An overcast layer of clouds viewed from above
USO	United Service Organization
walk away	Slang: easily leave behind

Printed in the United States
by Baker & Taylor Publisher Services